Over the past number of years, leadership teams and individual Church in Ireland. As we have worked together, local churches in radically different contexts, north and south, urban and rural have found themselves hopeful once again, as we have discovered or remembered that God is using us in our everyday lives; we have been supported and challenged as we have worked out what it means to be friends to one another; and we have been strengthened because the culture change to which this book points is challenging and does, as Neil points out, demand perseverance. As we have engaged in this process in God's grace, we have seen transformation in individual lives and in local church cultures.

Scattered and Gathered is a wonderful resource as, with God's guidance and encouragement, we help one another to be 'whole-life disciples'. Read this book, but don't read it alone! Read it with church leadership teams and in discipleship groups, talk and pray and allow God's Spirit to use it not just to inspire (and it will!) but to act, and to keep going.
The Revd Dr Heather Morris, General Secretary, Home Missions, Methodist Church in Ireland

I have benefited from Neil's engagement with and understanding of culture for over twenty years. His piercing insight, clear thinking and passion for engaging with and retelling the kingdom story in our ordinary everyday workplaces has formed much of my own thinking in this area. *Scattered and Gathered* is an outstanding contribution to engaging the potential of every church member everywhere, every day. It awakens imaginative faith and provides practical tools that equip believers and church leaders. Essential reading for every leader who wants to unleash the local church to honour God in all the corners of culture!
Alan Scott, Lead Pastor, Anaheim Vineyard, California

Like me, many Christians had their lives turned upside down by the vision in Neil Hudson's *Imagine Church*: a community of believers being equipped to live as missional disciples in their everyday contexts. The challenge for leaders, of course, is how to sustain the vision over the long haul. In *Scattered and Gathered*, Neil describes how churches can do just that – not with new programs, but by reframing what they are already doing as disciple-making

opportunities. If you want to make disciples, but don't think you have the time, this book is for you!
Chris Lake, Director, Vere Institute, Boston

Many Christians still live under the misapprehension that only parts of their lives are spiritual – the churchy parts. This is an impassioned and persuasive deconstruction of that pernicious fallacy and an exploration of the relationship between our 'gathered' and 'scattered' times. This is a book for anyone desiring greater coherence and authenticity in their faith, and for anyone involved in church leadership wondering how to deepen the everyday discipleship of the people in their care. Neil Hudson has studied and lived his material and he writes with powerful conviction and clarity.
Jo Swinney, Director of Church Communications at Christian Publishing and Outreach, and author of Home: The quest to belong

This book is the fruit of a number of years of careful research and day-to-day experience. I can recommend it because I have seen the practical outworking of these ideas unfold in Neil's vibrant local church community, where people are being equipped to live out their faith on their own frontlines.

Neil shares his wisdom and offers both a challenge to the church and a practical manifesto to help us better equip the 98 per cent of Christians not in paid church leadership. This is a treasure trove of theological insight, biblical examples and practical ideas to transform your church.
Chris Lane, Church Leader, Langworthy Community Church, Salford, tutor and lecturer in Theology, St Mellitus College, and author of Ordinary Miracles

Inside the chest of every church leader beats a heart for the church to make an impact for the kingdom. The book you are holding is not a quick fix, nor the latest fad or programme assuring you of instant success. Rather, it is a guide for reposturing your church towards your town or city. Neil is a brilliant teacher. But he is an even better learner. This book contains incredible insights and lessons that Neil has picked from churches around the UK and, indeed, the world. Read and be inspired and challenged but, ultimately, be repostured.
Sam Jackson, Chair, Christian Leaders Network, Toowoomba, Australia

The local church across the United Kingdom finds itself in a moment of significant cultural change in how we conceive of discipleship and engage in mission. In an ever busier world, the changes demanded cannot be 'add ons' to an already bloated church life, they will have to find a place in the existing grooves and rhythms of worship, preaching, small groups and friendships. This book enlarges our vision of what that looks like and helps to navigate a way towards a different expression of being the people of God. Read it with rigour. Lead through the lens it offers. Practise whatever suggests itself with patience. Expect to encounter the reshaping of the Spirit.

The Revd David Thompson, Secretary, Council for Congregational Life and Witness, Presbyterian Church in Ireland

I have had the privilege of hearing Neil teach on 'frontline' mission. It is hugely stimulating. His writing is as good as his speaking and this book is truly radical in its implications.

Martin Charlesworth, Training Director, ChristCentral Churches

There is a present need for the church to rediscover afresh what it means to be the body of Christ that is both gathered and sent. Week after week we come together to worship before being sent back out to be Christ's followers among the people and places of our daily lives. This book looks at the implications of this for church leaders and how we ensure that all we '*do*' as gathered church nourishes, strengthens and equips people of all ages and backgrounds to '*be*' the church Sunday through to Saturday. Neil Hudson has been walking alongside leaders in a variety of contexts and church traditions for a number of years and this is reflected in the practical treasures of this book, which will stimulate, challenge and encourage people in church leadership.

The Rt Revd Rachel Treweek, Bishop of Gloucester

At the heart of this book is a vision of what church could be like; of how our gathered life as church can enable us to fulfil our identity as disciples in the whole of our lives – in our myriad contexts. But it is also immensely practical. Neil roots everything in a reminder that, throughout the Bible, God works out his purpose for the world through the everyday actions of his own people. The book is peppered with illustrations from the real lives of ordinary people –

from Kendal, to Boston, to Salford and Ireland. And it's realistic about the challenges for leaders in knowing that whole-life discipleship is not for a season or a moment in time, but is what each of us is called to as we learn the way of Jesus in our own everyday contexts. As we seek to renew the church, Neil reminds us that the answer to the prayer, 'Come, Holy Spirit' is not simply that our worship offering will be more enlivened, it is that the people of God can re-enter their scattered contexts with a renewed sense of resilience, creativity and boldness.

Debbie Clinton, Director of Renewal and Reform, The Archbishops' Council of the Church of England

In looking for a new book to take the whole-life discipleship agenda forwards and keep it to the fore, I have a tick-list of things that I would look for. I would want biblical examples and insights, real-life stories and applications, practical suggestions and lessons learnt when putting them into practice and, ideally, I would want all these things to come from someone who I know is actively applying them in his or her own church context. Neil Hudson's *Scattered and Gathered* ticks all these boxes for me.

I can see *Scattered and Gathered* being helpful for individual church pastors and leaders, leadership teams, groups of churches working together and even for whole denominations that are seeking to take the whole-life discipleship message forwards and I recommend it for all these contexts.

The Revd Ken Benjamin, Minister, Chichester Baptist Church, Baptist Union President 2019–2020

When I speak to church leaders about equipping the everyday saints in their congregations for their whole lives, mostly I see fear in their eyes. There is a lack of confidence in their authority to speak into contexts that are unfamiliar. What is it like to be a full-time mum coping with exhausting demands on body and the temptations of social media? What is it like to be a bank executive with the pressures of performance and managing an eclectic team? What can be done to encourage the store shelf-stacker who has no sense of agency, joy or meaning in doing that job? Neil Hudson provides a wonderful resource that answers all the questions: how, what, when, where, why, who? All done with the insights and experience of being a church leader. Every suggestion has been tried and

practised and the stories demonstrate what it looks like. There is a rich vein of biblical truth running through the whole book; and the creative description of scriptural stories that start each chapter are a resource in themselves. In the crowded field of faith and work books, it is sometimes hard to find something new, but Neil Hudson has prepared fresh material that will help churches when gathered to be more effectively resourced when they are scattered.
Kara Martin, lecturer, Mary Andrews College, Sydney, Australia, and author of Workship: How to use your work to worship God *and* Workship 2: How to flourish at work

Neil Hudson has been at the forefront of inspiring the church to grapple with the task of disciplemaking for many years. This book condenses the visionary insights, biblical imagination and practical ideas that have helped make this work so successful across a variety of denominations and in very different places. Important and timely, this book is essential reading for any church leader who wants to deepen his or her practice of ministry and help shape the culture of church life to make a real difference to the mission of God.
Dr Nick Shepherd, Programme Director for Setting God's People Free, Church of England

Scattered
&
Gathered

Neil Hudson

Scattered
&
Gathered

Equipping disciples
for the frontline

INTER-VARSITY PRESS
36 Causton Street, London SW1P 4ST, England
Email: ivp@ivpbooks.com
Website: www.ivpbooks.com

First published 2019

British Library Cataloguing-in-Publication Data
A catalogue record for this book is available from the British Library.

ISBN: 978–1–78359–992–9
eBook ISBN: 978–1–78359–993–6

Set in Dante 12/15 pt
Typeset in Great Britain by CRB Associates, Potterhanworth, Lincolnshire
Printed in Great Britain by Ashford Colour Press Ltd, Gosport, Hampshire

*Inter-Varsity Press publishes Christian books that are true to the Bible and that
communicate the gospel, develop discipleship and strengthen the church for its mission
in the world.*

*IVP originated within the Inter-Varsity Fellowship, now the Universities and Colleges
Christian Fellowship, a student movement connecting Christian Unions in universities
and colleges throughout Great Britain, and a member movement of the International
Fellowship of Evangelical Students. Website: www.uccf.org.uk. That historic association
is maintained, and all senior IVP staff and committee members subscribe to the UCCF
Basis of Faith.*

CONTENTS

PREFACE

For over a decade, I have had the privilege and joy of working as part of the team at the London Institute for Contemporary Christianity (LICC). The focus of all our work has been on inspiring and equipping Christians for the kingdom possibilities of their everyday contexts. The church has yet to see all that could be possible through Christians who have a renewed imagination for their Monday-to-Sunday contexts and a greater confidence around the difference that they could make on their frontlines – in schools, offices, shops, gyms, libraries, homes – wherever they are, seven days a week.

Over the years, the LICC team has developed a wide range of resources and teaching for Christians in their frontline contexts.[1] Some in our team have also worked alongside leaders of churches and denominations to support them in equipping their church communities for fruitful Christian living in the whole of life.

My work has largely concentrated on working with these church leaders and denominations, developing a vision and practice of whole-life disciplemaking at local church level. My book, *Imagine Church: Releasing whole-life disciples* (IVP, 2012), reflected all that we had learnt from LICC's initial three-year pilot project in this area. During that time, I worked closely with seventeen churches from different spiritual traditions, social and ethnic backgrounds, sizes and locations. Our shared aim was to discover what whole-life disciplemaking could look like in these different contexts, so that we could learn how to help churches.

We have not finished learning, but the principles and practices emerging from this project are now in formats that many churches can access. They also form the basis of the teaching and training that we offer through LICC's church team.

In the past five years, we have also worked with hundreds of church leaders across many different church traditions, both in the UK and overseas. Fresh insights have emerged, new materials have been developed, tested, shaped and reshaped. Through our learning hubs in particular, we have been able to accompany churches as, over time, they celebrate and affirm the whole life of the whole church in the whole purposes of God.

Thousands of churches have used LICC's resources and hundreds of churches have taken intentional steps to strengthen the relationship between their gathered and scattered lives. Many have shared their experiences and insights with us.

This book emerges from the work with these denominations, networks of churches and individual churches and leaders. It builds on the core concepts found in *Imagine Church* and takes the thinking further. It remains a work in progress, but we are confident that we can help any willing church to get started on a journey towards becoming a whole-life disciplemaking church.

We know many churches that are experiencing sustainable shifts in their church culture, but the forces against this movement are significant – from society, from myriad distractions, from numerous challenges to the church and from the ongoing legacy of the sacred–secular divide. We are not complacent about the challenges faced by churches that want to become whole-life disciplemaking communities, but we are encouraged. It is clear that the desire to equip people for their everyday lives is shared by churches from across the waterfront of traditions and social contexts. It is not only an evangelical focus, nor only of concern to churches of a certain size or in certain places; it's a shared concern, both in the UK and in other countries around the world.

That is why we are publishing this book at this time. Certainly, we want to share some of the more recent learning and invite more churches to press on in strengthening their scattered-gathered life, but we also sense that the Holy Spirit is inviting the church to pay attention to this dynamic. We are not alone in working and praying for the radical change in the culture of the church so that the imaginative possibilities of the whole of the people of God are released. We see ourselves as part of a growing movement that we celebrate and are glad to participate in.

One final thing may be worth sharing. Alongside my work at LICC, for a long time I have had a part-time, paid senior leadership role in my own church, together with a group of bi-vocational leaders. It's a church that has grown steadily over the years, never spectacularly in any one year, but enough for us to enjoy the richness that comes from new people joining the community. This is my place. For all the work that I am involved with in the wider church, this local church is the place where I continue to grow. It's here that I have learnt what it means to be a disciple, and what it means to belong to a church community that tries to shape one another in Jesus' ways, and what it means to be a leader who is concerned for the Monday-to-Saturday lives of a congregation.

All these aspects of life flow into this book.

INTRODUCTION: FOUNDATIONS FOR SCATTERED LIVING

It happened to me again last week.

Alison had moved 250 miles to an area she didn't know, to care for family, and she was looking for a church to belong to, looking for somewhere that she could settle. She had found a new job, moved into a new house and had few friends, but had a family that needed her support. She was, understandably, feeling apprehensive.

At the end of the morning service, I was telling her about our church community.

I explained that we were less interested in how she could serve us and more concerned about how we could help her to discover how God was leading her in this new phase of life, in light of the demands and opportunities that she would face now.

She listened closely, didn't say anything, merely raised her eyebrows.

She clearly hadn't expected to hear this.

She was a church veteran.

But this was unexpected.

This was new.

At least to her.

Maybe she hadn't had this sort of conversation before.

Maybe she thought that I would be more concerned about how she would fit into our church.

Maybe she thought that I would tell her about the groups she could join.

Maybe she thought that I would ask how she might like to be involved.

Maybe she thought that I would ask which of the gifts she had.

Maybe she thought that I would be glad to see her because she was another 'resource' to fuel the church's vision.

Maybe she'd had these sorts of conversations before.

Maybe.

Seeing clearly

Thinking about how our life as church together – our *gathered* life – can support people in the places where they already are – their *scattered* lives – is still a new approach for many. But it is vitally important.

It matters because too many faithful, hard-working churches are sleepwalking into decline.

It matters because too many church leaders are struggling under the weight of the demands of keeping 'the church show on the road'.

It matters because too many Christians see their everyday lives, their Monday-to-Saturday lives, as incidental to God's plans for the world.

It matters because there are still millions of people who have yet to understand that there is good news for them.

It couldn't be more important.

Leaders have to be fully persuaded by this, otherwise the scattered lives of the church will always take second place to the perceived significance of gathered church activities.

There is much evidence that when the gathered church engages in mission and service in the local community, it can make a real difference to people's lives. No-one is disputing that, but it has to sit alongside validating the difference that individuals make in their Monday-to-Saturday lives when they are not engaged in local church activities. If we don't, we make two fundamental mistakes.

First, we privilege only part of the mission of the people of God. We fail to appreciate all that could be possible if we released all of God's people to see how their lives could be wrapped into his purposes. And second, we make life more difficult for ourselves as church leaders. We have to work ever harder to recruit people's pressured leisure time for church-sponsored projects.

It makes sense to widen the emphasis of mission from *merely* 'gathered' to 'gathered *and* scattered' but most people need help to see how this applies to them. It's why Alison raised her eyebrows and was taken aback by my conversation.

As leaders, how can we help?

I think it starts by a determination to see people in a particular way. When Paul wrote to the Corinthians, he explained how he had learnt to see people differently:

> From now on we regard no-one from a worldly point of view. Though we once regarded Christ in this way, we do so no longer. Therefore, if anyone is in Christ, the new creation is here: the old has gone, the new is here!
> (2 Corinthians 5:16–17)

I know how tempting it is as a church leader to look at people 'from a worldly point of view'. I fall into that trap sometimes when I make quick assessments about how useful they may be to church programmes. Though I would never be so crass as to use that sort of language, I might talk of their potential or how they make new things possible for us or how they will strengthen the church or how pleased I am that they have joined us.

The truth is that, when I meet people who are 'in Christ', they are part of the breaking in of the new age, the new creation. They have been reclaimed. They are part of God's brilliant venture with his own world. They are valued by him, they are desired by him and they are full of wonder. As a leader, I need to slow down enough to appreciate all that God has done and is doing in and through them. They may never be part of the music group or the children's work or any of my plans. That's not the point. God has not added them to our church to be fodder for our rotas. They have surrendered to Christ, they are part of the new creation, and they need to see how this deep theological truth makes sense in their everyday lives. If I don't take the time to help them see this truth about their identity, how will I be able to help people like Alison develop a vision for their own lives?

I want Alison to see that moving 250 miles to support family flows out of her desire to serve God, that this is part of her 'ministry' at this stage of her life. She may have felt there was no other choice and may be tempted to regret all that she left behind, but this is part of her offering to God. The new job is a new opportunity to serve others, to bless new people and grow as an individual. I want to be part of helping Alison to see all this and more.

I also want this to be normal for a whole church. A large part of church leadership is helping to create a community out of a group of individuals, but it is not community for its own sake. It is so relationships develop that nurture, support and equip us as we serve God's purposes wherever we find ourselves. It's hard work. Persuading people to move from merely attending a church worship event to developing closer relationships takes time, but if we are determined to help disciple one another for frontline contexts, it is the only way it will happen. The simple truth is this: we cannot disciple one another for the frontline just by meeting for 60–90 minutes on a Sunday. We need better, stronger relationships than that if our life together as a gathered community is going to enable us to live well in our scattered contexts.

All this has deep consequences for my life as a leader. Helping people like Alison means that I have to become a certain kind of leader. If I'm distracted by the latest church trends, envious of other church leaders who seem to be more appreciated, or judgmental of the congregation because change doesn't seem to be happening fast enough, I will be unable to help Alison. In short, I have to learn to love the congregation who called me to minister to them, and I have to act that out in practical ways so my actions reflect this belief about the church: both gathered and scattered.

In short:

I need to see Alison in a particular way;

I need to see the congregation in a particular way;

I need to see myself in a particular way;

we need a renewed sense of vision.

Four foundations

LICC's Church Team has served many UK churches committed to becoming communities that form disciples for the frontline. In doing so, we have learnt much about avoiding abstract church-talk and communicating dynamic, foundational concepts in ways that are both tangible and inspiring.

In one sense they are not new, yet it is clear that a fresh expression of these convictions helps people to go deeper in their understanding, commitment and joy about the possibilities they point to. These foundations are each described in turn in Figure 1.

1. *A fresh way of seeing church*

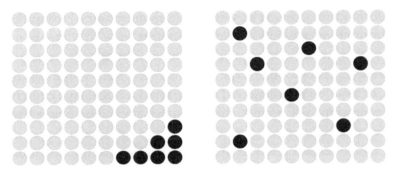

Figure 1: 'Gathered' worshippers (left) and
'scattered' worshippers (right)

The darker, more distinct dots approximate the number of people in the UK who worship in church once a month or more. It's a stark representation of the challenge we face. Equally, depending on how you look at it, it's also an opportunity.

On the left, we're a small, minority people.

We're also busy.

We care for the lonely, the elderly, the young, the unemployed, the debt-ridden, the spiritual searchers; we have a presence in schools, universities, colleges, hospitals and prisons; we support and connect with families, the bereaved, the addicted, the depressed, the hungry, the dispossessed. And most churches know that there is so much more that they could do.

Most churches do not struggle with a lack of opportunities to be involved in mission in their locality. They struggle with a shortage of resources, people, energy and money. The need is great, the people are few. When we look at the relative strength of many church congregations, it can sometimes seem overwhelming.

So how will we reach the UK?

On the right in Figure 1 are the same people seen from the perspective of where they are for most of the week – scattered throughout villages, towns, cities or beyond. They are there week by week, in touch with so many different situations and people. This is the experience of the vast majority of Christians: 98 per cent of Christians (those not in paid church leadership) will spend 95 per cent of their lives being the scattered church.

We are still a minority, but when we scatter into our everyday places, we are in contact with so many people and situations.

We may still be busy, but mission does not necessarily mean doing more.

Every week we are already in offices, voluntary groups, call centres, supermarkets, care homes, sports teams, job centres, banks, school classrooms, university administration offices, college canteens, social work teams, funeral parlours, hospital wards, cafés, local government offices and so many more places. We are there as the scattered people of God.

Of course, for that to lead to a fruitful outcome, two things need to be true.

First, we need to 'own' these places where we find ourselves. They may not be the situations that we would have chosen for ourselves, nor may they be the most fulfilling, but we are there. We may need to embrace the truth that we might be in these places because that is exactly where God wants us to be. It's been interesting to see how many people feel that they are not in the ideal situation, but when reminded that this may be God's place for them, they have been able to find a renewed sense of purpose and optimism.

Second, there is a call to be 'distinct' – to offer a distinctive alternative in our surrounding culture. Each week in our gathered worship, we tell a different story about the world. We sing and pray about a created world, a fallen world, a redeemed world, a world with an eternal future. This truth alone marks us out as different from many people. The words we use in prayer and songs remind us that we understand ourselves in a very distinct way. As scattered disciples of Jesus, we are different. The challenge is to live out the implications of that call.

But if, when we scatter, we 'grey out' and forget our distinctive identity, then the mission fails. This is the interplay between discipleship and mission. We need to learn how to grow as disciples of Jesus so that we will know how to live well in the many varied contexts in which we find ourselves week by week.

It's why both gathered and scattered church matter.

As we have reflected with people about the relationship between gathered and scattered church, some have assumed that we are pitching one against the other. It can be easy for leaders to hear us say that gathered church is not necessary or for worshippers to imagine that we are encouraging them to only concentrate on their scattered lives. Neither is true. In general, the activities of the gathered church have received so much attention to the detriment of the scattered church, but both aspects of the body of Christ are needed and are evident in practice.

Life is more complicated than a simple diagram might suggest:

- God uses the gathered church in mission and we are shaped as disciples in our scattered situations;
- equally, the experience of being in gathered church communities shapes us as disciples and we are able to engage in the mission of God in our scattered places;
- God is as present and active in gathered church activities as he is in the scattered places in which we find ourselves in – the art of the Christian life is discerning what God is asking of us wherever we are;
- sometimes our scattered lives will offer us the possibility of being with other Christians; sometimes we will be the only Christian there;
- we never stop being the church wherever we are.

It's just that these scattered places have been overlooked and so for too long we have had an inadequate understanding of the church in all its forms.

2. *A fresh way to describe discipleship*
Helping people to understand what it means to serve God's purpose in the whole of their lives involves reminding Christians of the significance of their identity as disciples and the significance of their everyday places.

The phrase 'whole-life disciple' is a shorthand way to describe that life. It reminds us that our core identity is centred on being a disciple of Jesus; it involves the whole of our lives and will last for the whole of our lives. For some, the word 'disciple' still has overtones of 'advanced Christianity' and is too easily connected solely to activities that feed our personal lives, rather than being intrinsically connected to our wider

lives: the world of work, family, leisure and so on. The fact that
the lordship of Jesus relates to every area of life through every
stage of life needs to be kept central for all of us, all the time.
Whole-life discipleship is a reminder that maturing as a
Christian is not something that simply shapes our private, inner
worlds; it affects, and must engage with, the whole of our lives.

In terms of encouraging people to identify their own
calling to mission, LICC has used the word 'frontline'. By this
we mean the everyday places where we naturally find
ourselves among people who don't know Jesus, places where
we might be the only followers of Jesus. We needed a
metaphor that could include everyone – from the youngest
to the oldest. As with all metaphors, it has its limitations.
Overall, though, people have found it a useful way to identify
the places where they feel God has placed them.

I'm convinced that the primary way we grow as disciples
is when we see ourselves serving God's wider purposes. In
other words, I don't think disciples are formed primarily 'on
retreat'; I believe they are formed in situations that demand
wisdom, perseverance and courage. These places are not
occasional exotic adventures; they are the everyday places
where we live out our everyday responsibilities.

Without these everyday places being firmly in mind, discipleship can become mere personal development. At the
heart of all that will be explored in this book are these two
central issues: how we understand our identity as disciples
of Jesus, and how we see our everyday places as places of
opportunity for the reality of God's kingdom to break in. It
is the way that disciples are formed.

3. A fresh way to imagine mission

Mission is the overflow of our relationship with Christ in the
places in which we find ourselves. It's less about deciding to

do new things and more about us acting consistently as followers of Jesus in our everyday places. When mission is abstract, disconnected from particular places and particular people, then it always seems intimidating. But when people accept that God has placed them in their specific situations, at least at this time, then they are able to explore more freely what mission might look like.

Talk of mission, however, can be vague. For some, it can suffer by becoming simple 'niceness'; for others, it is only defined by evangelism. A more helpful framework for missional living is one that highlights the range of actions that mark out a disciple of Jesus. This way of living will be generally true at all times in all places, though the expressions will be specific in a given place at a given time as lived out by a particular individual.

An extended exploration of a framework for missional living can be found in 'Fruitfulness on the Frontline', a course that developed from work that my colleagues, Mark Greene and Ruth Walker, did with people reflecting on their experience of serving God on their frontlines.[1] This framework is presented in the form of 6Ms (see Table 1 on p. 12).

Talk about mission doesn't always leave people feeling encouraged. The more frequent responses are twinges of guilt, being reminded that you could do more. But the framework of the 6Ms is not like that; it encourages people to recognize the significance of the things that they have already been doing. Because God is always at work in and through us, what we are already doing is an overflow of the life of Jesus. This is massively affirming as we all feel more motivated if we know that we are not starting from scratch.

There are challenges as well, but if we start with affirmation, people are better placed to face them. The first three Ms ('modelling godly character', 'making good work' and

Table 1: The 6M framework

Modelling godly character	As we allow the fruit of the Spirit to be evident in our daily lives, it becomes clear that often these virtues are unusual. For example, in an age of fast-moving distraction, patience shown to others can be countercultural and can offer a window into a different life, a different set of motives.
Making good work	Doing everything for Christ is both part of our worship and part of our witness. The way we engage with daily tasks becomes the space in which we practise our 'ministry': to God and the world.
Ministering grace and love	Going the extra mile is costly in time and emotional energy, but it is part of the call to live sacrificially for others – in the very ordinary day-to-day contexts we are in.
Moulding culture	We know that life is not perfect. We are called to live resiliently in the world as it is, not as we would wish it was. There are times, however, when, regardless of our official position in an organization, we can change how things are done in our bit of that world. When we can, we should.
Mouthpiece for truth and justice	Most of us are not able to do this on a national or international stage. Yet, every day, when we combat lies, snuff out gossip or work for justice for others, we are living out some of the central values of the kingdom of God.
Messenger of the gospel	There are times to explain why the message of Jesus is so compelling. We can describe the difference he has made to our lives and how we see everything differently because of him. The gospel message needs to be explained. Actions are not enough. Words are needed to tell the bigger story that God invites everyone into.

'ministering grace and love') call for a consistency in life. The challenge is to grow in this life of consistency. The people we live with and work alongside need to see that the out-working of our faith happens in the everyday, normal joys and challenges of life, and that in these places we are reliable.

The final three Ms ('moulding culture', being a 'mouthpiece for truth and justice' and a 'messenger of the gospel') call for courage in these places. Being willing to change how things are done, take a stand for what is right and true, and to speak about the gospel and Jesus all take courage. It's always easier to blend in with the existing culture, not make ripples, not to be true to what you believe to be true. This, for many, has been the main challenge.

Put together, though, the 6Ms offer people a sense of how their lives can make a contribution to the mission God calls them into on their frontlines.

4. A fresh way to introduce change

When you become convinced that change is necessary, it is inevitable to want everyone to get on board. That desire can mean a leadership team spends a lot of time trying to explain its intentions and dealing with the inevitable resistance that happens when people realize change is going to happen. Disappointment and disillusionment often develop in the wake of something that just seems too difficult.

We know that an organization's culture takes time to change fully. It's not that changes cannot be made, it's just that it takes longer for those changes to be integrated naturally into the life of a community. Many researchers would suggest something in the region of five to seven years.

But the wonderful irony is that change which needs to be sustained over a long period of time can start immediately.

'One-degree shifts', the small changes that over time will result in deeper change, remain a powerful communication tool to make long-term change seem less daunting. The goal of all these small changes is the deeper culture shift that needs to take place in many churches.

But they need to begin now.

There will never be a perfect time.

There is only today.

The shape of this book

Cultivating a meaningful dynamic between our gathered life together as a church and our experience of living as disciples of Jesus in our scattered places requires us to be clear regarding three fundamental questions.

- What does it mean to be a disciple of Jesus?
- What practices enable these disciples to develop?
- What sort of leaders are needed for these churches?

This book has been shaped by these core questions. It is ordered in this way because I want to start by focusing on the central task of the church. I believe that the church's primary vocation is to make disciples of Jesus. If we can keep that at the forefront, then we can explore how our life together as church communities serves that goal. And if that's clear, then the role of leaders becomes much clearer too.

But it is important to note that I am talking about people becoming a certain type of disciple. I have encountered so many people who have testified to the way their lives changed once they recognized that their everyday life, their 'sleeping, eating, going-to-work, and walking-around life' (Romans 12:1, MSG), fits into God's plan for his world. These epiphanies happen in all sorts of ways, but they are often defined by a sense of joy at a new purpose, a renewed enthusiasm for the places where they work and live, and a desire to know how to serve God faithfully in all the different stages of life. It has been absolutely liberating, and more people need to experience this good news for themselves.

As a church leader myself, it's what I want for everyone who belongs to my church community. But, too often, the inner life of the church – rotas, services, meetings and more – become the urgent things and so get most of my time and attention. And that is the challenge. It's easy for church life to take on a life of its own and become a resource-hungry machine that means Christians don't feel fruitful unless they are serving that machine.

We need to break this pattern.

If our hope is that all worshippers will see the significance of their own lives as part of the mission of God, our life together as a church community has to change. That will have implications for church leaders – lay and ordained, paid and unpaid, full-time and voluntary. If Christian leadership is fundamentally about service to the wider body of Christ, there needs to be a clarity about the qualities needed by leaders if the outcome of all that leadership is to be the fruitfulness of others. Leadership is vital, but we need to know what the fruit of all our leadership should be.

A quick scan of the above three issues is enough to show that it's impossible for one book to be exhaustive about any of these areas of concern, let alone all three, but what will be highlighted are these truths:

- disciples are called not only to be loyal to Christ in their personal, private lives but also to live out the implications of the lordship of Christ in their everyday, public lives;

- churches that support and nurture these sorts of disciples are communities that keep people's everyday contexts in the forefront of their planning of week-by-week ministry;
- leaders of churches able to serve these churches are consistently curious about the lives of those they minister to – they ask certain kinds of questions, they act in certain kinds of ways and they see their own ministry through certain kinds of lenses.

Hopefully, by the end of this book, it will be very evident that, while this can sound obvious, basic and fundamental, many churches need more than good resources; they need a fundamental change of culture.

Most church leaders have always wanted people to live out their whole lives as authentic followers of Christ. Unintentionally, though, many have ministered in ways that suggest the *really* important acts of ministry happen when they are church-sponsored activities, the engagements of the gathered church. It's why many church leadership meetings are still dominated by items of business about gathered church activities. Reflections on worship services, issues around the building, fears about attendance, conversations about pastoral concerns, these are all worthy of discussion, but there are other, even more important issues that often get sidelined. Many church leadership teams still do not ask how their gathered church life is helping people in their scattered lives, nor how they need to respond as a church community in the light of these scattered contexts. Churches that do not take this into account are missing so much.

Most worshippers who spend much of their week away from gathered church activities know that being a Christian means there is a responsibility to live, act and speak differently, but they often do not know what that might mean in their particular setting. For some, that lack of clarity is allied to the sensitivities of identifying oneself as a person of faith in a society that increasingly suspects faith is the source of many problems, not the cure. So, it is not hard to understand why some struggle to know how they can live as confident disciples of Jesus in their own circles of family, friends and colleagues. We may know that we are the scattered church. We are sometimes not so certain as to what that can mean in practice.

Who this book is for

My hope is that this book will help those who have responsibility for the gathered life of the church; that it will stimulate them to see how churches and individuals can put whole-life discipleship and disciplemaking into practice.

I want the book to be of practical help to those who are ordained as well as the countless thousands of volunteers who care passionately about their church communities. With that in mind, I am hoping that you might have some context where you can talk about the issues raised here with other people.

One of the enjoyable consequences of writing *Imagine Church* was becoming aware of how people used the book. Some leadership groups made the book a focus for a year's conversations, working slowly but methodically through it together. In other places, it was only read by the primary leader, who then was able to develop the material in church. Other leaders used it in their leadership networks, discussing it over lunch, trying to make sense of how the principles might work in their contexts.

There was one church leadership team made up of people who didn't read much for leisure, so they had little enthusiasm when the pastor suggested reading it together. It felt too big a commitment. So, ingeniously, he ripped chapters out of the book and handed the torn pages round in a bid to make it feel more manageable. I never expected that to happen.

I wish I could have listened in on all these conversations. I'm sure a second edition would have been required to reflect new insights. I am hopeful that this might offer another chance to take those conversations a little further, whether or not you decide to rip the chapters out!

The shape of each chapter

Each chapter begins with a retelling of a New Testament event. I know how easy it is to miss the grittiness and messiness in biblical stories that have been read many times. I hope that these short imaginative retellings will cause you to pause and rethink how God and his people engaged with their world in the exciting days of the earliest church, so that we might see how he continues to do so today.

They also serve as an introduction to some of the themes that will be explored in each chapter. I hope that, most of all, they remind us all that the work we are engaged in here is not simply about organizational reordering. This is so important. Leaders are 'shepherds of God's flock' (1 Peter 5:2). We are given the responsibility of caring for, guiding and shaping a community that does not belong to us. It is God's. We may be shepherds, but there is a 'Chief Shepherd' (1 Peter 5:4) to whom we are all accountable. Leaders need to communicate with and take instruction from the Chief Shepherd. Prayer and the Bible, both ignited by the Spirit, remain our primary resources.

If we are not careful, we can take on the efficiency obsessions of our own age and so treat people as projects rather than working carefully with them so that they can serve the Lord with their own gifts, in their own places at this particular stage in their lives.

The Bible reminds us that God works out his purpose for the world through the everyday actions of his own people. That sounds easier to discern than sometimes it is. At times, we struggle to make sense of what is happening and what our response should be. The fact that we see this within the pages of Scripture may be of some encouragement to us.

To help that process, alongside biblical reflections, the book includes stories of people and churches, insights that have developed out of many conversations with church leaders, and some suggested practices that might help the work move from the realm of the theoretical into the practical lives of church communities.

My hope is that all this triggers ideas for what might be possible in your particular situation.

Praying hopefully

This book is a call to action. It's not hard for us to name the challenges the church faces, but what is needed is the hope that we can make changes which will mean people like Alison will be able to grasp a wider purpose for her own lives as disciples.

What follows could sound very pragmatic or even formulaic. I believe that there are things which need to happen, actions to be taken that help the scattered lives of worshippers to have a new vision for their lives. The desire for change demands that changes are made.

If, however, we just tweak church services or imagine that training small group leaders more effectively will be enough, we fool ourselves.

We need fresh vision. We need to see people like Alison differently and help them see their own lives differently. We need to see our churches differently. We need to see what it means to be a leader differently.

More than that, we need God to do what only he can do. Perhaps that's why Paul shared his prayer for the Colossians at the beginning of his short letter to them. He would offer them an amazing vision of the all-encompassing nature of Jesus and he would instruct them about their everyday lives, but first he shares the prayer.

It's a prayer that we all can pray:

> We ask God to give you complete knowledge of his will and to give you spiritual wisdom and understanding. Then the way you live will always honour and please the Lord, and your lives will produce every kind of good fruit. All the while, you will grow as you learn to know God better and better.
>
> We also pray that you will be strengthened with all his glorious power so you will have all the endurance and patience you need. May you be filled with joy, always thanking the Father. He has enabled you to share in the inheritance that belongs to his people, who live in the light. For he has rescued us from the kingdom of darkness and transferred us into the Kingdom of his dear Son, who purchased our freedom and forgave our sins.
> (Colossians 1:9–14, NLT)

So may it be.

Part 1

SCATTERED ON
THE FRONTLINE

As Jesus walked beside the Sea of Galilee, he saw Simon and his brother Andrew casting a net into the lake, for they were fishermen. 'Come, follow me,' Jesus said, 'and I will send you out to fish for people.' At once they left their nets and followed him.
(Mark 1:16–18)

When Jesus called his disciples to follow him, everything changed. These young fishermen saw something in Jesus that was absolutely compelling.

Compelling enough for them to set aside whatever plans they may have had for their own lives.

Compelling enough to be given a new direction in life.

Compelling enough to be trained in new skills.

Compelling enough to follow a teacher with a clear vision of what life was about.

I have a deep conviction that the primary calling of any church is to become a disciplemaking community. Our common task is to help one another hear that compelling call of Jesus.

Therefore, church leadership is primarily about enabling a community to create whole-life disciples.

The work of leading gathered churches, which form confident disciples when they scatter, has surprising outcomes:

- it makes the Christian faith credible to those who do not yet believe;
- it helps Christians see how their ordinary lives really matter to God;
- it leads to joy – for everyone involved.

Part 1 of this book unpacks what this looks like in practice, when we are committed to help one another discover the richness of following Jesus: as gathered church and as scattered disciples.

It's foundational work and it's where we begin.

1. THE INVITATION TO WHOLE-LIFE DISCIPLESHIP

Our conversation drew to a close.

There was a pregnant pause.

I waited.

She said yes.

She understood little of what would follow.

How could she?

I'd told her that she was known, that her ordinary life in the back end of the world's greatest empire had been noticed and counted as significant. Her life of buying at the market, cleaning houses, repairing clothes, cooking meals, playing with children, catching up with local news, avoiding troublesome demonstrations, paying her dues and preparing for her own wedding celebrations all added up to something quite remarkable.

She struggled to believe that.

I doubt that she ever thought her life mattered to anyone outside her family and her fiancé.

But on this day, she heard me say that this life, her life, was about so much more. The very ordinariness of a young woman's days mattered.

And though, to many watching her, nothing would change, for her, everything would change.

Because she believed me.

She allowed herself to be enlisted into a different story, one that she could never have expected. A story that would change everything.

So it began.

Five words that opened up a new future: 'I am the Lord's servant.'

Five words began the adventure.

Many people read biblical stories like this believing that they could never experience anything similar in their lives. They keep these stories in the realm of 'church-talk'; encouraging, moving even, but unrelated to their everyday life experiences. It's tempting for people to assume that God speaks like this only to particular people, never them. They just get on with life.

But if we pull the lens back on the text just a touch, we will see that, for Mary, the implications of the message of what would happen in nine months' time would be worked out in ordinary time, in ordinary places, among ordinary people.

After turbulent early years, her life would continue with everyday tasks and regular responsibilities. She would continue to be part of town life, surrounded by friends, family and acquaintances. By the time the circumstances of her son's birth were fading in people's memory, her life would just continue to look ordinary.

To everyone except her.

She would remember the beginning; she would be there at the end.

One particular woman.

One particular life.

One particular experience.

One particular moment.

One particular response.

Except her response becomes a kind of template for all of us who try to help one another to live as disciples of Jesus. Like her, we also need to offer a personal response to God's call on our lives. We need to surrender to the claim of Jesus on our lives. We need an awareness that he calls us to serve his purposes in the reality of our own lives.

We all start in the same place. We will end up having different responsibilities, different areas of gifting, different abilities and different experiences. But we all begin by working out what our response will be when we hear the most basic of calls that Jesus ever makes: 'Come, follow me.'

If we surrender to that call, our lives will never be the same again. He begins a new story in us, with us and through us.

From time to time, though, we can be tempted to forget what that call actually entailed. So let's be clear.

The fundamental truth about what happened when we surrendered our lives to the lordship of Jesus, is this:

we didn't enlist God to help us with our lives,
he enrolled us to be part of his cause.

This is the foundational truth about discipleship. Everything that happens from this point forwards will mean that we have the chance to learn what it means to become part of God's big story and what it means to live as a follower of Jesus in our bit of the world.

It's the most basic of calls and carries the most life-changing consequences – for everyone.

It's where we begin.

Together as church we help one another to understand what it means to be the 'Lord's servant' in our contexts. As leaders with particular responsibilities within local churches, our task is to help the whole church family grow in what that means.

This is crucial work. If we do not have a shared confidence in the power of the gospel, then, at best, we will be assuming that people share a solid understanding of what it means to be God's people, when in truth it may be much shakier than that. Fundamentally, equipping people to live fruitfully on their frontlines assumes that they have a relationship with the living Lord. Without that, we will always be talking at cross purposes.

All this raises the question: how do we help people to come to that realization?

Awakening to the call to follow Jesus

It's easy for people to confuse an invitation to follow Jesus as merely an invitation to get involved in church activities. If that's the case, it's no surprise so many turn the invitation down. But, every now and again, someone encounters the real thing.

They hear the good news about Jesus not just as an invitation to get involved in religious activities in their spare time but as something that makes sense of the whole of their lives. When that happens, it changes everything. It's what happened to Simon.

Simon was like many of his non-Christian friends growing up in a town experiencing post-industrial decline. He was a young man who wanted to make something of his life, and a big part of those plans involved getting married.

In time he completed the trickiest part of the plan. He fell in love with someone who was more than happy to marry him. He was less confident about the next move: organizing a wedding.

So he did what anyone who doesn't belong to a church does: he made an appointment to meet the local vicar. Nobody in his family or his circle of friends ever went to church and he had low expectations, but they wanted to have a 'proper wedding' and so wanted to get married in church. He certainly wasn't looking to become a Christian. Any idea he had of Jesus was distinctly hazy and seemed of no relevance to his own life.

After meeting with them, the minister agreed to marry Simon and his wife-to-be, but with the proviso that they would come to a number of church services beforehand. That was something new for both of them. Those first early visits to church included many things that left Simon cold, but what did impress him was hearing the gospels being read and the sermons that connected all Jesus did with the issues of life they were facing in their town.

He was intrigued by the relevance of the gospel to the world in which he lived. In hearing about the kingdom of heaven for the first time, he heard good news for his world. As he said:

I was struck by how applicable and useful it all was. Even though it scared me a little, I could imagine trying to live out the meaning of Jesus' parables in my office or among my friends. It was good news for neighbourhoods in which crime and heavy-handed policing had led to riots and a besetting hopelessness. It was recognizably good news for people I knew.

What Simon had heard was a whole gospel for the whole world, and he was drawn into becoming a whole-life disciple. It led to a profound conversion of his heart, to baptism and a commitment to live as a disciple of Christ.

When people like Simon see the real connection between the gospel and their experience of life's reality, it is not hard to see why the good news becomes compelling. It begins when those who are sharing this good news are fully aware of how world-shaking it is. There is a fundamental need for us to keep on being fully aware of all the implications that arise from being addressed by this central figure in the gospel. If we have accepted that Jesus is the central focus of the story of the world, then we will need to keep on emphasizing that the invitation is to pledge allegiance to a new Lord. That lordship has to be seen as relevant to our whole lives.

As Dorothy Sayers wrote in her famous essay 'Why Work?' so many decades ago: 'How can anyone remain interested in a religion which seems to have no concerns with nine-tenths of his life?'[1] If the gospel we invite people into is only linked to the 'religious' bits of life, there can be no surprise that the invitation is declined. But if the lordship of Jesus is understood as being good news for the whole of our lives, it comes with an urgency that will at least be taken seriously.

Reawakening to the call to follow Jesus

In some ways, we might feel that it's easier to deal with people like Simon than with people who have spent a lifetime as churchgoers. Simon saw the whole-life implication of the gospel and the demand it would make on him. For those well versed in the ways of the church, it is easy to dismiss the whole-life claims of the gospel and encouragement to live with confidence on one's frontline as fanaticism.

Being in the church for a long time may be the real problem. It's a strange truth that you can be part of many church communities for years and, as long as you don't let down your guard too far, but carry on serving, it's quite possible that no one will ever ask you if you are still growing in faith or trusting God in daily life. Sometimes we have allowed our churches to be communities of such acceptance that there is no space to challenge one another. Consequently, in some cases, it's easy to become engrossed in church activities and yet be spiritually lethargic.

As leaders, how do we make sure that we minister out of a hopeful expectancy that people will encounter God, rather than a resigned frustration that believes nothing will change?

As worshippers together, how do we spur one another on to keep growing in faith and the expectation that we might be involved in the answer to our prayer, 'may your will be done on earth (in this place: my place, my workplace, my wider family, my neighbourhood, my sphere of responsibility) as it is in heaven'?

There is no cookie-cutter approach to this spiritual awakening. The primary reason for this is because it is all down to grace. 'Grace' is the gentle word that 'helps us to remember what sort of God we are dealing with: one that would never coerce us, and is humble enough repeatedly to invite, appeal, and even plead with us.'[2] For those of us longing to see people come to life, that means we need to exercise grace-filled patience. But it also means we will continuously believe that there are new possibilities for everyone.

It's why hearing Jesus' commission to his disciples is so helpful.

Jesus' commission and our challenges

The climax of Matthew's Gospel is intriguing, but it's easy to miss some of the finer details in the light of the Great Commission: 'Go into all the world'. A closer reading offers help to those who feel they are in churches that have lost, or never had, an understanding of what it means to be disciples on the frontline.

> Then the eleven disciples went to Galilee, to the mountain where
> Jesus had told them to go. When they saw him, they worshipped
> him; but some doubted. Then Jesus came to them and said,
> 'All authority in heaven and on earth has been given to me.
> Therefore go and make disciples of all nations, baptising them
> in the name of the Father and of the Son and of the Holy Spirit,
> and teaching them to obey everything I have commanded you.
> And surely I am with you always, to the very end of the age.'
> (Matthew 28:16–20)

Jesus was with his disciples consistently for three years. They
seem to have shared much of their lives together, giving up
work to learn from him and to travel around the country with
him. Even so, his final words in Matthew's account reflect the
same challenges that we have in church communities twenty-
one centuries later.

I see four challenges here that reflect the work we are
engaged with in local churches. They are the challenges:

- of a mixed group
- to our imagination
- of specific contexts
- of new responsibilities.

We will explore them one by one.

1. The challenge of a mixed group

> Then the eleven disciples went to Galilee, to the mountain
> where Jesus had told them to go. When they saw him, they
> worshipped him; but some doubted.

That final little clause, 'but some doubted', has caused
commentators to cover acres of paper trying to explain what

was happening. Regardless of what they were doubting, or indeed why they were doubting, it's interesting that at least some of these first eleven disciples were doubting. His call was to all of them, the whole of this little band of men, some of whom still had grave doubts about what was happening and their places in it all. Matthew's climactic call to global Christian mission starts in a very uninspiring place.

It's a challenge to our tendency to judge people we worship alongside. '*"Doubting worshippers"* are Jesus' material in mission', so we shouldn't be 'perfectionist about who can be used by Jesus for his missionary purpose.'[3]

This picture of the first disciples reminds me of so many churches that I know. Definitely a mixed group: a mix of worship and doubt. As it was in the beginning, I suspect it will be for all time. There was never a golden age when everyone was equally enthusiastic about the adventure of following Jesus. We start with what we have, not by wishing we had something better.

It's tempting to feel that if your church community was made up of more spiritual people, all would be well. It's easy to become a judge of the church community you are called to be a part of and to serve. We have to start where we are: these people, in this place, at this time. Some will be fervent worshippers, some will be determined doubters. Most will be a mix of both.

Jesus commissioned them all.

So should we.

2. The challenge to our imagination

Our eyes can slide over the imagination-blowing introductory words of Jesus to these faltering disciples: 'All authority in heaven and on earth has been given to me.'

It's easy to think that this refers to a statement of doctrinal belief or a more general faith-statement, but to these disciples, it was a real challenge to their imaginations. Everyone in that circle knew that, ostensibly, nothing was different from how it had been two months earlier. The Romans were still crucifying troublemakers, the Jewish authorities were still disapproving of the general population, the land was still not their own and things still looked bleak. Jesus' intention was for his disciples to understand the full significance of the cross and resurrection for their whole lives and for the whole earth.

This challenge to our imaginations has always been part of the work that we offer to one another as Christians. There has been a long-standing temptation to reduce faith to private, personal, inward matters, for family and household alone. If it had not been needed in the earliest church, we probably would not have had epistles such as Colossians. That imagination-awakening text helped those Christians to see the implications of the lordship of Christ for the whole of life.

The poem-hymn in Colossians 1:15–20 offered the first generation of Christians a picture of Jesus as being at the centre of God's plans for the whole world, but also overseeing every detail of the universe, holding it all together. This Jesus, this saviour, could never be limited to their private lives; he is simply too big and his actions too wide for that to be the case. The message of the whole New Testament is that, amazingly, God is concerned about our whole lives but, far more than that, he wraps them into his plans for the future of everything. It is, of course, either preposterous nonsense or the most astounding news ever shared. To settle for a purely private faith is, simply, to settle for too little.

This took faith to believe then. It still does.

He [Paul] is invoking and celebrating a world in which Jesus,
the one through whom all things were made, is now the one
through whom, by means of his crucifixion, all things are
reconciled. This is not, of course, the world that he and his
friends can see with the naked eye. They see local officials
fixing allegiance to Caesar. They see bullying magistrates,
threatening officers. They see prisons and torture. But they
are now invited to see, with the eyes of faith, the eye that
has learned to look through the lens of scripture and see
Jesus.

Like an apocalyptic vision, this mystery-revealing poem
offers a glimpse of another world, a truer world than the
violent and brutish world of paganism then and now.[4]

I cannot imagine it was any easier for Paul to help the
Colossians see this than it is for us in London, Lima or Lusaka.

This is still the task that we are constantly re-called to
engage in. It will be welcomed by some, such as Simon, the
young man wanting to get married, because it means that
everything makes sense. There is a centre around which
everything is held. For others, though, it might be more of a
challenge. It means that the compartmentalization of our
lives needs to stop. It means that this faith we hold to will
affect our whole lives. Everything becomes important, everything can be offered to God. Our whole lives get caught up in
his story, his plans.

The challenge for us as we worship, preach and pray is to
find ways to help one another see the remarkable lordship of
Jesus, this much bigger world.

3. The challenge of specific contexts

Jesus said: 'Therefore go and make disciples of all nations.'
There could never be a one-size-fits-all approach to mission,

because Jesus sends all of us into different locations with different cultures and different histories. Over the years, mission agencies have become proficient at preparing people to make these moves into different overseas cultural contexts. Where we have failed is in helping one another in our specific, local contexts. After all, there can be a world of difference in the conversations that barbers can have with their customers and those that are acceptable, or possible, between barristers and their clients. As Mark Greene has often said, each workplace really is a 'foreign country'. Each has its own different, mostly unwritten, rules about what is expected and acceptable. We can help one another to be prepared only if we understand more about the cultural contexts each of us is involved with.

It's important that when we are using the language of discipleship, we help people realize that their discipleship is always worked out in their own contexts. I'm not the only church leader who has spent hours trying to locate the course that will do the work of discipling a whole congregation. At one time I thought courses like that existed. I'm older and wiser now. I am fully persuaded that the art of discipleship is firmly linked to the context in which we find ourselves. So, the learning we engage with must be context-specific, rather than course-driven. At each stage of life and in each particular situation in which we find ourselves, there are different challenges. As Lucy Peppiatt says, there is a concrete-ness to this life of discipleship:

> The place where we learn to trust him is in the concrete circumstances of life. We cannot put the words of Jesus into practice in the abstract, but only in our everyday lives and in our real relationships. And it is only in these places that his words will really be tested.[5]

It is in these places, our everyday contexts, that we learn what it means to be a disciple. It is in these places that we discover how to live out the implications of the life of a Jesus-follower.

My definition of a disciple is this: people who are learning the way of Jesus in their contexts at this moment.

It doesn't cover everything that could be said, and it's just one definition among hundreds, but one advantage of this as a starter-definition is that it puts Jesus centre stage. Being a disciple is not primarily about learning the ways of the church or the ways of cultural Christianity. It's far more radical than that. We are called to learn the ways of Jesus.

It also reminds us that this is a continual action. We never get to the end of the process of learning because our context always keeps changing. There is an ongoing necessity for wisdom to be applied to whatever latest situations we face.

Finally, it suggests that we learn in company with others. This life of discipleship is not one for rugged individuals. We learn from, and with, others around us who are, in turn, learning the way for themselves.

If we are going to help one another grow in these everyday settings, there is an obvious challenge: we will have to know one another's daily contexts better than we may have done in the past.

4. The challenge of new responsibilities

The first disciples were commissioned to make disciples of others. They were to introduce them to the realities of Christian faith, teach them all that Jesus had taught them and see the expansion of this faith.

How do we help one another be part of this movement when we may be part of churches that have not been challenged to see their Christian faith in this way, but have been content to be church-attending, privatized Christians? This is the most common situation many face and the most difficult, so there can be no easy answer. Culture takes time to change if it is to be long-lasting. Some of the groundwork for this change was explored in *Imagine Church* and some further, necessary changes will be explored as we go through this book.

I think it starts with someone being willing to name the core vocation of the church.

We are a disciplemaking body.

Too often we worry more about the growth of the church, or the aesthetics of worship, than we do about the outcome of all our activities together.

We can enjoy being together and not help one another to grow as disciples.

We can see our congregation grow and not help one another to grow as disciples.

We can serve our local community and not help one another to grow as disciples.

We can be very busy and not help one another to grow as disciples.

But, if we help one another to grow as disciples, then it is very likely that we will enjoy being together, we will grow, we will serve in so many ways and our busyness will be fruitful. We just need to make sure that we are able to keep this central to our life together.

It starts by having the courage to outline the church's purpose and then to act as though that were true. We are called to be a community of disciplemaking disciples. It means that we will help one another know how to live our whole lives for the glory of God and know how to encourage others to live in the same way. As Graham Cray wrote, 'The ultimate test of the fruitfulness and authenticity of any church, irrespective of its style or tradition, is the quality of the disciples it makes.'[6]

It takes a whole church to grow a disciple

Our call to follow Christ is also an invitation to become part of the church. This body of fellow disciples can keep us accountable to the commitments we make. Together we can grow in our desire to follow Jesus. This can never be the task of a single church leader. It cannot even be solely the task of a church leadership team. It has to be the task of the whole church community.

It's why the gathered life of the church is so important. It is in these contexts that we have the opportunity to be formed, shaped, nurtured and supported in our life of discipleship. Our gatherings may be limited in time, but the fact that we know we belong to one another and we have a circle of support when we serve God's purposes in the wider world is priceless. This is the body that can help us stay committed to the call of Christ.

These communities do not need to be perfect to do this work, but they do need to know that this is the calling of the church. We are called to 'live together with him [Christ]. Therefore, encourage one another and build each other up' (1 Thessalonians 5:11).

For any who are feeling a little beleaguered at this point, let me encourage you. You may have too many things to do already, and you may know that this work of helping one another grow as disciples works best in small gatherings of two or three people. How will you be able to do this for everyone?

The simple answer is: you won't and nor should you try.

But you can start with one or two. You can meet for an hour weekly, fortnightly or monthly for a set period and help one another understand what God is doing in and through your lives. You can ask good questions, reflect on Bible passages and pray for one another. You can encourage and listen. You can share wisdom. You can help one another grow as disciples who are learning the way of Jesus in their context at this moment.

Responding to the call of Jesus takes a lifetime to work out. The commitment will be tested in the everyday contexts of our frontlines. It is these specific locations that offer us the opportunities to work out the particular implications of being a disciple of Jesus. But it is being part of a church that is committed to growing whole-life disciples that will make it possible for us to stay faithful to Christ and bear fruit.

The life of discipleship begins with a personal response. It continues and is sustained by recognizing that we are part of the body of Christ.

IN PRACTICE
Helping one another learn the way of Jesus
We want to help committed but sometimes doubting congregations live fruitfully with renewed imaginations in their particular frontline contexts.

We want them to carry their responsibilities as disciples of Jesus well.

This does not happen accidentally.

It needs intentional actions.

But there are actions we can all take.

Live it out myself as a leader
It begins with the most obvious, and some days the most difficult, truth. I have to recognize my primary vocation as being a disciple. I have to allow myself to be captivated by the prospect of following Jesus in my particular context.

It's not enough to begin by talking about what needs to happen to 'them'. It has to be about our lives, our commitment to Christ, our practice on the frontlines of our lives.

It's why some church leadership groups begin their business meetings with the opportunity for some of the group to share what they are 'learning about following Jesus in their context at this moment'. It keeps them clear about the reason for all the conversations that will follow.

Keep prayer central

Disciplemaking movements have sometimes found themselves coming off the tracks when they have become more about the tools and behaviours of discipleship rather than enjoying a life with God.

In the desire to see people come to Christ and grow as disciples, it is easy to think more about the techniques than the fact that, ultimately, this is a spiritual battle for the hearts and minds of all of us. This battle takes place foundationally in prayer. Prayer is both the basis of our ministry to one another and the means by which our support of each other bears fruit.

To pray well for people entails knowing them. In most churches, it's possible to invite four or five individuals or families each week to share their frontline prayer concerns with a church prayer group or, indeed, a whole church community through some form of social media. Too often our prayers can be for 'the church' in general, rather than for the individuals who are the church specifically. We need to pray for both aspects of the church: gathered and scattered.

Explain clearly

If churches are going to move from a gathered-church emphasis to a scattered-church equipping model, it will take a thoughtful process that is shared by all. I'm cautious about processes that are essentially done to people. I don't think there should be hidden agendas in the church, among brothers and sisters. At the same time, if a vision is launched with bells and whistles, then more might be promised than can be delivered. Perhaps it is enough that everyone knows, 'this matters to us and you might notice some changes over the next months. We would love to know if they are helpful to you.'

Extend an invitation

We need to have the confidence to invite people to follow Christ, whether that is for the first time or as a reminder that we are called to a lifetime of whole-life discipleship. Because there is always more to learn, the invitation is not a judgmental one, but a reminder that we are wrapped up into God's purposes for his own world. We need the courage to invite people into this adventure and the willingness to recognize that, on occasion, people may decline that invitation.

For some people, the invitation may be the opportunity they have been waiting for – one that allows them to join the adventure of living their life in and for the kingdom of God. We don't want them to miss that moment and we don't want to lose the privilege of being part of the process whereby they say 'yes' to all that lies ahead.

2. DEVELOPING VISION FOR EVERYDAY DISCIPLES

The children were asleep.

'I won't be long,' I whispered to her as I slipped out.

I was glad I'd brought the cloak. It was cold. The wind was blowing through the trees. It would soon be winter.

Across the town, through the town-gate, turn left towards the lake. My eyes get accustomed to the dark. Not easy to see, too easy to trip, but good for listening. Everything seems louder in the dark.

I found the tree we had agreed to meet under, and I waited. Nothing to be anxious of. This was my area. I'd known it since I was a boy. I ran around here, grew up here. It's my place, I'm known here.

Then he came.

Suddenly feeling uncertain of myself, I opted for formality. I could imagine my colleagues wincing when I said 'Good Teacher'.

He didn't look like much, this young, wandering preacher, but you couldn't deny, there was something about him. Something we lacked. Something I lacked. Something I wanted.

I'd thought I would have been the one making the running in the conversation. I was used to that. But not here. Not with him. Within minutes he'd tied me in knots with talk of wind, breath, kingdom, birth, gift.

But I know he was right. I didn't understand it all, but I glimpsed the truth.

I was someone – I could be someone.

I had a history – I could have a future.

I'd been born into a people – I could be reborn into a new people.

I had a role – I would need to rethink it all.

I had a reputation – I might lose it and gain something more.

Back in the house, everyone was asleep.

I lay awake.

All I could hear was the wind outside.

On so many occasions Jesus is simply enigmatic.

Intriguing.

Appealing.

Surprising.

Shocking.

But, most of all, unexpected.

His talk with Nicodemus in the shadows circled around the imagery of wind, breath, life, spirit, the Spirit. It must have been enough to make Nicodemus's head whirl. But Jesus was unapologetic about his approach.

He knew about Nicodemus's hope that the kingdom of God would be established and everything would be put right. He was clear, though, that this would only come if Nicodemus was ready for a new start, a new birth into a new family.[1]

The result of that new birth would change everything. Just as the natural wind was unpredictable, so it would be with anyone born of the Spirit (John 3:8). These people filled with

God's wind, his breath, his Spirit, would act in ways that would never be predictable. Those reborn into a life with God would have their horizons filled with the possibilities of the kingdom of God, even if, maybe especially if, that clashed with the expectations of the rest of the culture.

That's what it meant to Nicodemus. Years later, together with Joseph of Arimathea, under cover of the night, they both risked their reputations by asking Pilate for the broken body of Jesus, and then prepared it for burial with over thirty kilograms of spices (John 19:39). At that point they were unaware how the story would end and we lose sight of them after the resurrection. But at least at this point, Nicodemus is ready to spend time, money and reputation on Jesus. He had clearly seen something different in him. Something had clearly changed in him.

This is what it still means to be a disciple of Jesus.

Helping people to see clearly

Disciples need to have a new vision for their own lives. As leaders, we want them to be able to see that their everyday lives can flow into the wider mission of God. We want them to live confidently in their frontline places.

If that is going to happen, they will need:

- a clearer sense of their identity as Christ's people;
- a clearer sense of their involvement in God's plans.

Before we explore this, one comment is necessary, especially for those in positions of church leadership. All that follows can easily be described as what 'they' need. In truth, it's what 'we' need, regardless of position or responsibility. We are all first and foremost disciples.

A clearer sense of our identity as Christ's people

We need to get a bigger sense of what mission can involve in order that we can be both encouraged about what we are doing and challenged about what we might do. But there is danger here. It's the danger of activism without relationship. Marianne Thompson, reflecting on John 15, highlights the issue:

> Strikingly, Jesus does not exhort his disciples to bear fruit; rather, he exhorts his disciples to remain attached to him, the source of life. Elsewhere in the New Testament, the fruit that is borne indicates what is within a person; here [John 15] fruit is produced as a result of the life of the vine. As Lesslie Newbigin aptly puts it, 'The fruit is not an artifact of the *disciples*; it is the fruit of the *vine*. It is the life of Jesus himself reproduced in the lives of the disciples in the midst of the life of the world. The presence of fruit is the visible evidence of the fact that the branch is part of the vine.' Hence, Jesus' exhortation 'Abide in me.'[2]

Mission can only flow out of our relationship with Jesus.

This is the link between the classic spiritual disciplines handed down through the generations – study, prayer, fasting, solitude, meditation and so on – and that life lived on the frontlines of our everyday lives. These disciplines help us grow into our relationship with Christ. They become the way we clear space, mentally and physically, to enable us to become more attentive to the reminder that God gives us, that we belong to him and are loved by him.

Often there has been an artificial divide between spiritual maturity and mission. Congregations may have divided themselves into the 'spiritual-disciplines-camp' and the 'mission-camp'. The obvious truth is that we cannot engage in mission unless we have a strong foundation of knowing that we belong to Christ and are aware of what that means in our lives. Nor can we just concentrate on our own spiritual development if it has no outflow of mission. At best that looks like selfish personal development.

When Paul was trying to encourage Christians in Galatia to keep going as followers of Jesus, he reminded them that their experience of the Spirit would enable them to live counterculturally. They would be able to avoid the behaviours acceptable within the culture of the Roman empire that did not reflect the values of the kingdom of God. And they would learn to respond differently in their social relationships (Galatians 5:13–15; 19–23, 26). Paul knew that walking in step with the Spirit would help them to respond creatively to the situations they faced. The work of the Spirit still enables us to respond differently in our workplaces, our family relationships, our friendships and neighbourhood responsibilities. These are the arenas, the frontlines, in which our discipleship is played out.

Creative living on our frontlines flows out of the life offered to us by the Spirit through Christ. Activism without abiding will simply lead to exhaustion. The call is to receive this life of God, this wind, this Spirit.

One of the responsibilities of leaders of church communities is to ensure that the church grows deeper and grows wider. People need to mature as disciples and they need to know how that life affects our everyday situations.

A clearer sense of our involvement in God's plans

As leaders we can encourage people to take mission seriously by helping them connect their everyday lives with the bigger purposes of God. This interaction is how we encourage people to see their own lives as having greater significance than they otherwise might have expected.

The gospel story began when the Word became flesh. At that point, all our desires to talk about God in neat speculative categories were turned upside down. The early Christians made the extraordinary claim that we can know what God is really like because at least one generation touched the incarnate one. The infinite became finite, took on flesh and walked on our streets and ate our food. And we were introduced to God. Even as God limited himself for our sakes.

That truth about the incarnation became the blueprint for God being at work in his own world. It's the glory and frustration because incarnation is about limitation. The glory is the particularity of how God came. The frustration is that this involved an inevitable limitation.

Jesus came as a man, not a woman.

He came as a Jew, not a Gentile.

He came to Judea, not Gaul.

He was a tradesman, not a synagogue ruler.

He lived in the first decades of the first millennium, not at the beginning of the third.

He was limited and particular.

It's how God chose to work.

It is a similar situation today. We can't be everywhere and everything to everyone. But it is glorious because it is about the particular. It's me, here, now, with you, with these opportunities and these challenges. That's how God chooses to take our lives and weave them into his purposes. The more we can take that seriously, the more we can resist the ancient heresy that neuters our imaginations about what God thinks is *really* important.

It means that our everyday relationships, our everyday plans and our everyday actions matter. Nothing offered to God is wasted.

'Whatever you do' – preparing the accounts, changing the nappies, baking the bread, clinching the deal, teaching the class, writing the new software code, policing the estate, rehousing the immigrants or interviewing the prospective students – 'whether in word or deed, do it all in the name of the Lord Jesus, giving thanks to God the Father through him' (Colossians 3:17).

This is our task together. To help one another see that it all counts. That being a follower of Jesus means we bring everything under his lordship, however small those things may seem.

> It all matters. That someone turns out the lamp, picks
> up the windblown wrapper, says hello to the invalid, pays
> at the unattended lot, listens to the repeated tale, folds the
> abandoned laundry, plays the game fairly, tells the story
> honestly, acknowledges help, gives credit, says good night,
> resists temptation, wipes the counter, waits at the yellow,
> makes the bed, tips the maid, remembers the illness,
> congratulates the victor, accepts the consequences, takes
> a stand, steps up, offers a hand, goes first, goes last, chooses
> the small portion, teaches the child, tends to the dying,
> comforts the grieving, removes the splinter, wipes the tear,
> directs the lost, touches the lonely, is the whole thing.[3]

It all matters. But to really help people, we need to offer some answers to the question, 'Why does it matter?' Otherwise we just have clever slogans.

Paul's letters have far more guidance to slaves than to masters. It's not that he doesn't know the power that householders held and the temptations that they faced, but he spent more time writing for the household slaves. It makes sense that he would do so. There were numerous slaves in the empire and they seem to have been quickly included into the early church communities.[4]

The slave passages (Ephesians 6:5–8; Colossians 3:22–25) do not make easy reading for us today. We might have wanted Paul to be less quiescent with the social hierarchy, more willing to radically denounce the unjust structures. It's clear that he sees freedom from slavery as something to go for if it's possible (1 Corinthians 7:21–23) and offers a really nuanced perspective on master–slave relationships in the church in his letter to Philemon. But he doesn't recommend slaves to riot and overturn society; he does something more significant. He subverts society's expectations.

First, to people with limited freedom, power or influence, he offers a picture of how everything can be seen differently if they offer their everyday activities to the Lord in worship.

Instead of just working for their masters, they are to see their everyday tasks as being for the Lord (Colossians 3:22). This is what people find so encouraging to think about: why their very particular tasks matter. If we can help those who work as cleaners to see their vacuum cleaner as an instrument of worship, they can begin to believe their work to be richer than anyone could imagine. Their labour might not be recognized by others, but it is certainly received by the one who called an ordered creation into being.

If accountants can believe that it is primarily the Lord they are serving as they prepare their customers' tax returns, they may realize why the time has been well spent (Colossians 3:22–23). This is one of the ways we reflect the Creator's design for beauty, order and provision.

If grandparents, an essential part of the family team caring for young children, see their walking to and from the school gate along with the after-school homework help as part of 'doing the will of God from your heart' (Ephesians 6:6), there may be a deeper pleasure taken in it than the natural joy they may already feel.

It all matters because, fundamentally, it is one of the ways in which we serve the Lord.

Second, it all matters because the Lord will reward those who do work in these subordinate positions (Ephesians 6:3; Colossians 3:24). Paul doesn't go into detail about what that reward will be nor when it will be given. He was just certain that there would be a reward; that the way we live in even the most uncongenial of circumstances is never overlooked by the Lord.

Third, it all matters because, by working faithfully, slaves could be a blessing to their householders. Timothy is urged by Paul 'to teach and urge them' that slaves who follow Jesus are not to take advantage of believing masters. These masters are brothers and sisters in Christ and 'dear to them' (1 Timothy 6:1–2). Whether their master is a fellow-believer or not, they could work in such a way that they become a blessing to those around them.

It all matters because when slaves demonstrated that they were trustworthy, they made the gospel credible and plausible (Titus 2:10).

And lest all this gives the impression that everything will always run smoothly, Peter reminds slaves that their experience of painful injustice allows them to walk in the footsteps of Jesus (1 Peter 2:18–21). Injustice does not have the final word.

Three ways to see this in practice

Exploring these passages is not without its difficulties. We are distanced from them in every conceivable way and, used inappropriately, they can justify wholesale abuse of workers' rights. But, on occasion, people hear the teaching and find the relevance to their own lives. As they tell their stories, you see the modern-day equivalents of people offering their work to the Lord and finding a new freedom, of being determined to serve those they work with and refusing to let the hard times rob them of the chance to act as agents of unpredictable blessing.

It was a Saturday in Kendal, the market town in the beautiful Lake District. The room was full of church leaders and people wanting to explore what whole-life discipleship would mean to them. One lady had already explained to the group that she was a one-woman cleaning business, servicing the grand houses on the shores of Lake Windermere. She explained that she hardly ever met her clients. Job lists were left on the table for her. Her money was paid into her account. Her clients could quickly become anonymous.

She talked of the temptation to take shortcuts, ways of giving the appearance of a job well done, but not done. She was challenged by the idea that her work mattered in as much as she could offer it to the Lord.

As she left, she thanked me for the day. I asked what had particularly helped. Her answer was moving: 'You gave me back my dignity.'

She'd come to the day knowing she was a low-paid, dispensable worker. She left knowing that what she did mattered. Really mattered.

Sometimes you get the privilege of meeting remarkable people when you least expect to. It was a rainy night in Boston in the USA. I'd been speaking to church leaders at training events and the day was coming to an end after supper in a church member's home. Walking back to where I was staying, I chatted to one of the people who had been there. Her name was Ruth. Spontaneously and entirely naturally, she began to share stories that showed how things can change when you believe that everything matters to God.

Ruth works in the human resources department of local government. A vibrant Christian, Ruth has long believed that her work setting gives her the privilege of working for God's glory. As she interviews people, along with the score-card exercise everyone uses, she is praying for discernment. She knows that work for some applicants can be the way a life is remade and given new dignity. She is praying that she won't miss this opportunity.

It was not out of character for her, then, to become aware of the injustices that some local government cleaners were experiencing. One day she asked her boss if he would allow her to find out what was happening. Perhaps understandably, he was less than keen. In his eyes Ruth's job involved files and notes and the occasional interview. Her request to go and work alongside the cleaners for a day was at best unusual. But his objections were no match for an African-American Christian woman with justice on her mind.

She was introduced to the cleaning crew as the newest member of the team, and she experienced life as a cleaner. Their job was to be invisible and efficient. On a rainy Tuesday, they had to keep the City Hall's entrance dry for the local dignitaries to walk through while being as inobtrusive as possible. They were unseen, unvalued functionaries.

As lunchtime approached, they led her to the basement where, surrounded by broken furniture and heating pipes, they unpacked their sandwiches and had their 30-minute break. When Ruth asked them why they had to sit there, they explained it was all that was provided for them.

'Not any more,' she told me, with a massive grin.

The next day, she reminded her boss that the human resources department had responsibilities for the well-being of their employees and that they needed a dining area that reflected some dignity for these workers. It was found.

Ruth has no doubt that she has the opportunity to change the expected customs of her workplace. She knows that she is the child of God and is determined to live and work with that sense of identity at the forefront of everything she does. She's another Spirit-filled person working in unpredictable ways, ways that reflect the kingdom of God.

My third example happened much nearer to home. I knew that Ann had been struggling at school for a long time. She was a good teacher; she'd been told that enough times by colleagues and through appraisals. She loved teaching, but had struggled with the demands that had been made on all the staff when a new senior leadership team was appointed. At Christmas, she told me that she couldn't take much more and the situation was causing her sleepless nights. She had decided that she would resign at Easter. It was the hardest decision she had taken in her working life. She felt a failure and wondered why God had allowed it all to happen.

Easter came and we talked together on the Sunday after she had left the school.

ME: *How did it go?*
ANN: *It was the best day I've had there.*
ME   *[laughing]: Yes, I bet you were glad to go.*
ANN: *No. I don't mean that. It was a brilliant day.*
ME: *Why? What happened?*
ANN: *There were a few of us leaving and all the staff were*

gathered, having drinks and nibbles. I'd decided what I was going to do beforehand. The head said some nice things about us, but it was a bit awkward because of all the difficulties they have caused so many of us. Then she asked if we would like to say anything.

I was the last to speak. I thanked various people and said the expected things and then took a deep breath and asked if I could pray for them. I explained that I wanted them to be blessed and I believed God could do that and, without stopping, began to pray for the school, the children and the leadership team. It wasn't long but I could see that the head had tears in her eyes and she came and put her arm on my shoulder.

I wanted to do it because I wanted to leave well. I have been so hurt, but I didn't want to leave with resentment. I wanted to bless them. It was the only way I could think of doing it then.

ME: *Wow!*

Ann's not a super-confident evangelist. She's a teacher, burdened by unreasonable demands, who was determined to act differently – to be a blessing, to subvert the norm, to be unpredictable.

These stories are not very unusual. There are many of God's people acting like this, often unheralded and mostly unknown. These people have a clear sense of their own identity and a clear sense of how their lives connect with God's desires for his own world.

The question for church leaders is how is it possible to help people get this sense of purpose in their own lives? In many ways, the whole of this book tries to answer that question, but there are ways to begin.

IN PRACTICE
Uncover what is happening

The primary task of church leaders, long before they try to plan what should happen, is to discover what is already happening. It would have been easy to have missed the three stories above. The people involved did not set out to tell me what was happening. They are not the sort of people to blow their own trumpets. They told their stories because each of them was in a place where there was time for them to tell me what was happening and I was willing to ask and listen.

My hunch is that church leaders miss so many things that would encourage them enormously if they slowed down enough to listen. We have our hopes and plans and spend time trying to explain them so that others will get on board. We try to motivate people to see what might be possible. Yet, right under our noses, there are remarkable stories of the grace of God being lived out in the complexities of ordinary life. I fear we miss too much.

In practice, how do we help people to discover why their lives matter to God? We learn to ask good questions of one another. There follow two examples of how to do that.

Understand examples of fruitfulness

Some people just 'get' what it means to be a whole-life disciple. Their stories are compelling and encouraging to others. It's interesting and important to understand why they get it. It would be worth spending time with them to understand what has formed them as disciples.

- Are there things in their story that would help others?
- What did they experience?
- Who or what influenced them?
- Who taught them and what were they taught?
- Who or what encouraged them and how did that happen?

The outcomes of a conversation like this could help shape the ministry of a whole congregation if something similar could be offered to others.

Every congregation is 'God's field' (1 Corinthians 3:9). Therefore, each congregation can become a fertile place in which disciples can grow. If you already have fruitful disciples growing in your field, you need to find out why that is happening. The seeds for a bigger harvest may already be present in your own church family.

Help one another hear about their frontlines: 'This Time Tomorrow'

When churches begin to explore what it means to be a whole-life disciplemaking church, they invariably introduce time in their services for 'This Time Tomorrow' (TTT) in some form or other. It's very likely that you have already introduced this to your church.

This is the opportunity to allow someone to answer some form of the following questions in public.

- Where will you be this time tomorrow?
- What will you be doing?
- Who will be with you?
- How can we pray for you?

The significance of this goes beyond the value to the individual. It allows a congregation to get a feel for the spread of its own influence. We hear about the different contexts in which we find ourselves and the ways we are seeking to serve there. We also give a sense of significance to the 'ordinary'. In any congregation, there will be a small minority who are doing things that are perceived as interesting or significant. Most will be more mundane. This is where we can spark one another's imagination to see how the mundane can become the arena for the significant.

Churches that have done this have found that there are two common reactions. Initially, it is eye-opening and people love listening to these stories because they are interesting. In time, however, it is difficult to sustain and so it stops. Of course, it's fine to allow for changes, but if we stop because we have grown bored of listening to one another or because there does not seem to be much to report, then something fundamental has gone wrong. We have either lost the sense of wonder at each other or have lost the sense of wonder at the lives we lead. If people are to believe that their lives can make a difference, we need to give dedicated time to hearing about these lives and then to praying for them.

If you haven't used this as part of your gathered times, then begin. It sits easily within the prayers of intercession for churches that have periods of structured prayer. Equally, in churches that have a history of testimony, it would fit naturally within that tradition.

There are variations on the TTT theme.

- One church uses credit-card-sized pieces of paper asking the questions of TTT, which can be placed in a basket during communion, so that people can take someone else's and pray for them during the week.
- The questions can become the basis of conversations at all-age services or Messy Church gatherings.
- They can become the natural questions that we share with one another over coffee. They will help people to recognize how seriously we take one another's frontline contexts and the support we are willing to offer one another.

TTT is a way to hear one another, but if it is just something that happens from time to time, it will not lead to the change that could be possible. The hoped-for outcome of organizing people to speak publicly about their everyday contexts is that this will become normal for people when they are not in formal gatherings. We cannot support one another if we do not understand one another's contexts. We cannot encourage one another to learn the way of Jesus in our contexts if we don't know anything about those contexts. TTT could provide the stimulus for new conversations across a congregation.

However you choose to hear one another, make sure you do. That wind keeps blowing, you might just hear it.

3. DISCOVERING THE JOY OF FRONTLINE MISSION

I don't need to tell you.

You could say I know men.

I've heard their promises. I've listened to their anger. I've heard the door close behind them. I've felt the absence of men. I've been defined by them.

So I don't easily get taken in. Not now. At one time I might have been easily flattered. But who wants to flatter me? At this stage of life. Someone with my life.

But hear me out. I've met a man.

I know, I know, but he's different.

He's confident and attractive. Brazen even. I'm old enough to be his mother and, at first, I felt like giving him a piece of my mind when I thought he was coming on to me. Like I don't know what happens to women at wells. I wasn't born yesterday.

You could say I know men.

This one is a teacher, but not like any I have met before. He was unafraid. Unafraid to debate with me. Unafraid of answers that I thought might throw him. Unafraid of what the village gossips would say about him. Unafraid of his reputation being dragged through the mud. Unafraid of me. Unafraid of my past.

I've been telling everyone, and he came when we invited him to come and stay with us. He walked across the boundary to our place. He's here – in our village. Come and meet him. He seems to know who we are and what we need and where we've been.

I think this could be the one. I know we've thought that before, but I really think he's the one we have been waiting for. I think this one will lead us out of the mess we're in. There's something about him that is so irresistible. He makes you believe that all this could end differently. That all this might mean something. The others are saying he's the one that will save the world.

Come on, all this can wait, come and meet him.

He's the one. The real deal. Come on, don't hesitate, don't miss him.

You could say I know men.

I do.

But let me tell you, this man knows me.

There was something faintly comical about the whole scene.

We don't know where the disciples had gone, but we are told that Jesus was tired.

Maybe he had had enough of the twelve-man team and wanted some time alone.

Maybe he asked them all to go into the town to get some food.

Maybe they wondered why it took twelve men to get thirteen lunches.

But that conundrum would have been nothing compared to their confusion when they got back and saw him speaking to that woman in that place at that time. Maybe they shuffled their feet, looked at one another out of the corner of their eyes, not wanting to ask the obvious questions: to her, 'What do you want?' and to him, 'Why are you talking with her?' (John 4:27).

Then, as she went to tell her neighbours that they needed to come and see this man, he tells them that he doesn't need the food that they have brought. 'I have food to eat that you know nothing about' (John 4:32).

Once again they are left perplexed. Someone else must have brought him food.

Meanwhile, the woman has gone back to her village, her neighbours and friends, and persuaded them to come see Jesus, and then they have persuaded him to go to their village. He does and stays there two days and many become believers (John 4:40–41).

That woman knew she had a responsibility to share what she had experienced, but the challenges facing her were enormous. There was the challenging frontline reality of turning up with a Jewish teacher in her Samaritan village; there was the challenge of wanting people to trust her when they just saw her as a 'woman with a past'; there was the challenge of Samaritans being presented with a new understanding of the future: 'there is a time coming when you will worship the Father neither on this mountain, nor in Jerusalem' (John 4:21).

This was not an easy frontline. But that was the context she invited Jesus into.

And he went.

He still does.

Embracing frontlines

When I have used the picture of the dots (see Figure 1 on page 6) in training sessions and explained that the potential of the scattered people of God only works if we 'stay distinct' and 'own the place', I've been surprised how many people have told me that they struggle with these places – their everyday places. So many feel that if they could be in a different place, a more promising place, then they would be able to serve God much more successfully. I understand what they mean, but it's important to remember that much of the Bible was written by, for and about people who felt that they were in the wrong place at the wrong time with the wrong people.

There was never an easy place to live as the people of God. They survived in Egypt, the wilderness, the under-threat land, the contested land, the corrupted land and the Babylonian exile. They returned to live under various forms of occupation until the days of the earliest church when they were dispersed among the greatest empire the world had ever known when Christianity would have been seen, at best, as a sect for disgruntled Jews. There was never an ideal moment or the ideal place.

There still isn't.

But when we help one another embrace the frontlines that we find ourselves in, then we can help one another know how to serve God there, even though they may feel unpromising and, at times, uncomfortable. When we do help one another do that, we find it involves joy.

The joy of affirming frontlines

One of the dangers in encouraging people to embrace their frontline contexts is that it can feel like a duty rather than a joy. For everyone, leaders and worshippers alike, it can be seen as another thing to do on a lengthening list of Christian demands.

There is no doubt, for some it is challenging, but we mustn't lose sight of the fact that this emphasis offers a renewed joy in ministry for leaders and adventure in living for those willing to discover what God might do on their frontlines.

The pull of the prevailing church culture, where church-sponsored events get all the attention, where the vision and plans of leaders trump anyone else's passion, where we only concentrate on recruiting people to the activities of the gathered church, is strong.

Leaders who help people to discover fruitfulness on their frontlines need to keep reminding themselves why it's worth it. It's about joy.

Rather than being a chore, affirming one another's frontline offers a chance to experience joy in at least three ways: the joy of resolving frustration, the joy of seeing people living out the attractive gospel, and the joy of recognizing God's missional creativity. Once that is seen in the lives of people close to us, we will want to continue to help people get a vision for their own lives.

The joy of resolving frustration

And there is plenty of frustration about.

Frustration like Jane's.

In conversation, she told a group how, when she was younger, she really wanted God to call her into 'full-time Christian ministry'. But God seemed reluctant to do that and, deep down, she knew it wouldn't have been right for her. She was left frustrated, though, so threw herself into the weekly activities of her local church as, to use her term, 'compensation'. She was wearing herself out, anxious that somehow she wasn't matching up to what she could have been if situations had been different. But everyone in the church was delighted. She was so helpful, so

committed, so dedicated. No one wanted to stop all her activity.
But it sprang from all the wrong motives.

There is frustration like Kevin's. A frustration fuelled by memories of the past.

As a church leader, he could look back to the time when everyone in his church community had all thrown their weight behind an overseas missions project. They were good days: united, committed, sacrificial. But now those days were just a distant memory. His church was a more dispersed community, busy with all sorts of other calls on their time and energy, seemingly distracted and less committed to mission.

His deep frustration was about how his church could love and serve the world around them when everyone seemed so busy, when everyone is so different from one another and when they all have different interests.

We need to keep two different aspects of mission running at the same time. We need the corporate expressions of mission, especially mission to the poor and the forgotten in our society. There is a desperate need for the ongoing work that church communities do week-in and week-out, up and down the country. Our work with the elderly and the young, the poor and the lonely, the seekers and the saints must all continue. The work needs groups of dedicated people if it is to be done. They provide a missional focus for those involved. We must not stop them.

And yet, we need to emphasize the fact that the scattered church is involved in far more places than the gathered groups of church can ever reach. We need to remind people that they are the living embodiment of the gospel, day by day, in relationships that will often stretch over years. And they are able to demonstrate all that the gospel means there.

Both matter. Both need to be highlighted. Both need to be resourced. Both need to be celebrated.

Because, if we do, we will address Jane's frustration of not being in 'full-time Christian ministry' because she will realize that she is. Every morning when she wakes up and goes to her office, she is entering her mission field.

It will address Kevin's frustration, too. He will see that his church congregation does have a united mission, but it is related to place rather than project. The congregation will be dispersed throughout his town and region, with a few wider-travelling outliers, so the impact of the potential mission engagement will be all the greater.

The joy of seeing the attractive gospel

One of the wonderful truths about following Christ as his disciples is that our lives can make the good news attractive.

As Paul's mission strategy of leaving behind small cells of disciples began to succeed, he needed to train the next generation of church leaders. Writing to Titus in Crete, he told him how to give the slaves a sense of their mission. Their task was to show that they could be trusted, so that 'in every way they will make the teaching about God our Saviour attractive' (Titus 2:10).

It's a fascinating way to view our own lives. Winsome living is missional living. Especially in contexts where you do not feel that you have much power. Steven Garber puts it like this:

> In the daily rhythms for everyone everywhere, we live
> our lives in the marketplaces of this world: in homes and
> neighbourhoods, in schools and on farms, in hospitals

and in businesses, and our vocations are bound up with the ordinary work that ordinary people do. We are not great shots across the bow of history; rather by simple grace, we are *hints of hope*.[1]

'Hints of hope' is italicized for emphasis in Garber's book. It's a great phrase. It allows us to be absolutely honest about ourselves and our opportunities. We are people who have been given a glimpse of a bigger sense of reality. Whatever caused our birth into this new story, whether it was a slow, growing evolution of awareness or an unexpected interruption of a life, we can carry this different view of everything and everyone around us into our everyday life. Often it will mean responding unexpectedly in the midst of ordinary life. Our lives in these commonplace situations matter because they are the places where we can live in such a way that is suggestive of a much bigger story.

I've long been challenged by the depiction of Father Joe Warrilow, the monk who was the spiritual anchor for Tony Hendra, a British satirist and writer. On meeting the monk, Hendra said:

> I knew I'd just met a man from whom would come none of the usual responses I'd learned to expect from priests. Some unknown fuel drove his engine. Gentleness bubbled out from the funny figure in the scruffy black robes like clear water from solid rock . . . I felt on the brink of learning an entirely new set of possible responses to the world.[2]

In my view, there can be few better commendations of another person. In a world where the usual responses can be predicted, what does it mean to act from a depth of Christ-likeness that is so compelling?

This way of life, this attractive, daring response to others carries far-reaching consequences:

David's neighbours knew him only too well. Cars pulled up at the house at all times of night, men knocking on his door, shouting, swearing, then speeding off. It was a residential street. It wasn't the neighbours' fault that this veteran drug-user had inherited his mum's house.

Thin, aged beyond his years, angry, scary. Most people gave David a wide berth.

Except Laura. Retired after a lifetime of teaching, she lives on the next road and has known of David and his family for many years. The only thing they had in common was they both had dogs.

They would pass each other walking their dogs and, because Laura is not easily scared, she would say hello to him, and speak to his dog. Although David was suspicious, in time he relaxed and they built a relationship that went beyond 'Hello, what horrible weather' [to David] and 'Aren't you a great boy?' [to the dog]. And she began to pray.

When she told us at church that she was delivering home-made cake and lasagne to David, we began to pray as well – for both of them. She told us about him, prepared us for the time she would invite him to join us, explained about the swastika tattoos and reassured us that he wasn't as scary as he looked.

One Sunday he came and was welcomed. He relaxed and came back again. Laura asked others to help and his doors were fixed and the garden tended. Someone offered him a new bed. Someone else gave him a carpet, and a sofa, and some pans.

He began to volunteer in the church café most days. He plastered someone's bedroom using skills that had been unused for years. He helped people train their dogs.

He carried on worshipping with us and began to believe the good news he was experiencing. And the neighbours asked questions.

Salvation was coming to a household.

There's a longer, deeper story here, but it's essentially a story of joy as we watch the effect of someone, backed by the active support of a church, making the good news of Jesus not just relevant but also intrinsically attractive.

Mission involves individuals ready to be a blessing and ready to act in ways that are unexpected. It's about counter-cultural acts of courage that meet people and situations as they are and a belief that things can change.

It's about brave humility.

It's about risk-taking.

It's about the wonder of a God who is with us on our frontlines.

The joy of recognizing God's missional creativity

Ultimately, the fruit of calling people to live faithfully on their frontlines will happen in ways that we cannot begin to predict. It's enough to be confident that this God of grace who invites us to surrender to the lordship of his Son is the one who creates possibilities that we can only marvel at. Knowing that relieves us of some of the pressure that we have needlessly borne. God is at work in these places; he is setting things up and he will wrap us up into his work if we are willing.

Sometimes it happens like this:

John works as the head of the music department at a sixth form college. He's a gifted musician but, more importantly, is a compassionate and passionate follower of Jesus.

When Susan retired from Christian ministry, she and her husband were the first residents on a newly built housing estate. She wanted to help the new estate to develop a sense of community and knew that they could be part of the 'social glue' that could build that there. So, she offered her services as a cleaner to everyone who came to live on the estate. That way she met everyone and was able to begin to build some form of relationship with them. It also meant it was easier for them, once a quarter, to host Sunday brunch for all the neighbours.

John and Susan don't know each other, but both know Martin.

One day John was telling me about how his week at work had been going and some of the long discussions he had had in the staff room with colleagues about whether or not the Christian faith was intellectually feasible. He told me about one staff member who would not let the conversation drop, even when John said that he had to leave to get on with some work. This colleague was argumentative, but in a way that suggested this was not purely an academic question for him. His name was Martin and we prayed for him together.

The following week, John asked me if I knew someone called Susan who lived about 6 miles away in one of the city's suburbs. In his ongoing conversations, Martin had mentioned another Christian he had met recently called Susan.

Apparently, Martin lives on Susan's road and had been to her house for one of their Sunday brunches and had spent a lot of time talking with her husband about faith and he was beginning to feel that maybe there was something about it all that he needed to take seriously.

I happen to know both John and Susan and it was great to know that two of my friends, unbeknown to each other, were being used separately by God to help one man explore the

Christian faith. I wonder how many times that happens without us knowing.

I think this might be one of the ways that the creative spirit of God is at work in and through his own people, who are willing to act in ways that are countercultural in order to enable others to see the compelling beauty of the gospel.

That particular story hasn't come to a conclusion yet, but that's not really the point. It's the wonderful way that God gets people's attention so that they can be aware of the fascinating brilliance of God's good news.

What it takes on our part is being committed to the challenge of the gospel, creative in the ways in which we enable people to experience this good news of Jesus and confident that this gospel connects with the whole of our lives and the deep questions we face. Mission involves individuals ready to be a blessing and ready to act in ways that are unexpected. It's about countercultural acts of courage that meet people and situations as they are and a belief that things can change.

It's about brave humility.

It's about risk-taking.

It's about the wonder of a God who is with us on our frontlines.

IN PRACTICE

Encourage new possibilities

On the whole, the challenge is not that Christians don't think there is a mission to be engaged with, it's just that too often they cannot see what it is, nor can they see how they could be involved. It seems too difficult, too alien to their lives, ultimately too daunting. They fear that they don't know what to do.

What people may believe they need most is answers. We
fear that if we begin talking with others about our faith, we will
encounter the killer questions that will leave us completely
stumped. The assumption is that everyone else is likely to
be more intelligent than we are and we will be left looking like
a speechless, gullible fool.

There are ways that we can be prepared for many of the
common objections to Christianity's claims about truth but,
ultimately, for most people these conversations will at best
present the Christian faith as a viable faith. It's not unhelpful
and, because the questions are the ones we ask ourselves, it's
a great thing to engage with the intellectual wrestling.

But there is more to living out the faith than just having all
the answers. The implications of being a disciple will flow out
of our lives in ways that we ourselves might even be oblivious
to. It will affect our responses and reactions to everyday conflicts,
distresses and joys. It will shape conversations about the future
and the past. It will mould the ways we approach strangers.
It may even impact the number of times we smile or are heard
laughing. It will be the hidden fuel that drives the engine.

So how do we begin to help one another see the possibilities?
It can begin by uncovering what is already happening in people's
lives and then offering encouragement about what could happen.

Offer a picture of what might be possible

Using the 6M framework of 'Fruitfulness on the Frontline' (see
Table 1 on page 12) helps people get a fresh perspective on what
they may already be doing and a new way of describing it. One
of the easiest ways to help people see this in action is to ask
them to identify how someone else is living out some of the 6M
characteristics of fruitfulness. If they can see it in someone else,
they are more likely to be able to understand what it would be
like for their own lives.

Encourage conversations that explore possibilities

These conversations can happen in small groups or one to one. They help people develop new imaginations for how their lives could be used, and are being used, for God's purposes. The best questions are open ones such as these.

- What would be the possible outcomes if we all lived as faithful disciples in our scattered contexts?
- What would happen to our workplaces and the institutions we belong to?
- Could people discover Christianity to be a compelling and viable faith because they have seen the church confidently living out all the implications of their faith in their daily lives?
- What would it mean to be fruitful in the ordinary places we find ourselves in most days?

It's important to allow these conversations to be 'What if . . . ?' conversations rather than 'Why it wouldn't happen' conversations. Would these conversations lead the church to pray with more confidence and faith?

Part 2

GATHERED FOR FORMATION

Now you are the body of Christ, and each one of you is a part of it.
(1 Corinthians 12:27)

This is one of the most poignant descriptions of the church in the New Testament. The body of Christ. It rolls off our tongues so easily, but when we stop to think about what that phrase might entail, it's astounding.

Groups of diverse people, gifted differently, in different parts of the world, with different experiences, all connected to the one head, together being the body of Christ.

Church becomes so much more than our Sunday gatherings or mid-week group programmes. This body, supporting one another, is a living, breathing demonstration of what Jesus is like.

It's true that lots of the time that demonstration is flawed, but every now and then you get glimpses of beautiful people doing brilliant things in difficult circumstances. Sometimes they can do these things together; most often they are doing them when they are apart.

But all the time they are the church, both in gathered mode and in scattered mode.

This section explores how our life together can sustain our life in these scattered church moments.

I believe that happens best when:

- we move from viewing church primarily as an event to embracing church as community;
- preaching connects explicitly with people's frontlines;
- worship helps us discern God's presence on our frontlines;
- small groups are places where we shape one another for life on our frontlines;
- we know we need more than organized programmes;
- friendship is prized.

Our life together as church should not primarily feel as though we have joined some impersonal training school. At its best, our life together as church provides the context for deep, transforming friendships to develop that support our life as disciples in the whole of our lives.

For some churches, this will involve a deep change in culture. This way of thinking may not be natural for them. What is valued may not be the adventures of the congregation on their frontlines. Their practices may not explicitly support frontline living. The changes suggested in this section are not minor tweaks; they are an entry point into a way of being church that will result in people being formed with a different sense of their place in God's mission.

4. WORSHIP THAT INSPIRES US FOR THE FRONTLINE

It took some of us a bit of time to get it.

I mean, we all were nodding and murmuring our agreements, but in truth, it only took Marcia to say, 'I have to say, I didn't really get what he was on about' for the rest of us to come clean and agree that we had also found it difficult.

Part of it was due to the time of day. It was the end of a working day. We aren't clever philosophers, we're local tradespeople: weavers, stonemasons, butchers and leather workers. Some of us work in households doing washing, shopping in the market or caring for children. Some of us are free people, some of us slaves.

So it took us a few read-throughs, but then the penny began to drop about what it all meant. When you're following Jesus surrounded by neighbours fascinated with pagan religions, alongside Jewish synagogues and Roman temples, it's easy to feel insignificant, but it's clear that Paul saw more.

He was stretching our imaginations.

It was all about Jesus. Not just the man in Judea, but the one who was there at the beginning of all creation, the agent of creation. The one who held things together, the one with the creative power that lies behind everything we can see and all the things we can't see or understand.

This is how we heard it being said:

We look at this Son and see the God who cannot be seen. We look at this Son and see God's original purpose in everything created. For everything, absolutely everything, above and below, visible and invisible, rank after rank after rank of angels – everything got started in him and finds its purpose in him. He was there before any of it came into existence and he holds it all together right up to this moment. And when it comes to the church, he organizes and holds it together, like a head does a body . . .

. . . all the broken and dislocated pieces of the universe – people and things, animals and atoms – get properly fixed and fit together in vibrant harmonies, all because of his death, his blood that poured down from the cross.

You yourselves are a case study of what he does.

(Colossians 1:15–23, MSG)

It began to dawn on us just how big this all was. Just how import- ant it all was.

We read it again and again and talked about how this changed everything. This good news is the best news. This good news is worth holding on to for life itself. This good news will see us through. This good news makes sense of everything: our work, our homes, our families, our hopes, our fears.

This is brilliant good news.

What if our gathered worship was able to spark our imagin- ations like that?

What if these times together gave us a wider perspective on God's actions for, and in, our world?

What if the shape of our worship times helped us to have new eyes for the places we find ourselves in most of the time?

What if we were to worship together in the light of our frontlines?

What might happen then?

It's interesting that when I've asked leaders the question, 'How does your church disciple people?', the answers vary so widely. There is a small minority who look quizzical at the question, but many will point to the small group system that runs in their church or a mentoring initiative that has been introduced or the more ad hoc conversations and visits that might be made by church workers. But rarely will leaders mention what happens in their Sunday gatherings.

That's interesting because it suggests the main time in the week when most of us gather is not seen as being central to our desire to become a disciplemaking community.

There are lots of reasons for that, but at the heart of it is that few people expect that it can happen there. I have to say, I think they are wrong. I believe that the regular act of gathering to worship together week by week can shape our expectations of how we see God at work in the wider world. If we are shaped by our experience of worship, then I believe that our Sunday gatherings can help one another live as full, whole-life disciples.

As a child, I grew up in the Salvation Army. Heavily influenced by the Holiness Movement renewal of the late nineteenth century, it had a strong emphasis on being different from the prevailing culture. Our attitudes to alcohol, gambling and sabbath-keeping had been forged in the mission to the working classes of industrial cities. It was clear: we were different.

Certainly my friends thought so. It wasn't unknown for them to stand on the pavement outside our house and sing

'Glory, glory, hallelujah!' as we drove off for yet another Sunday service. I was left with two massive theological problems: why did I have to wear a uniform and look so different (I longed to be able to go to a 'normal' church so as not to stand out so much) and why did God allow the sun to shine on Sundays when I wasn't allowed to play outside?

In reality, the second problem was less troublesome than it seemed. Our day of worship began at 10.00 a.m. and interspersing Sunday school or Open Air meetings (depending on your age) ran through the afternoon to the evening until we would all arrive home at about 7.30 p.m. thankful that another day of rest was over.

How times have changed. For many, if they can get to worship at church a couple of times a month, they feel they are winning the battle with the overcrowded diary.

But leaders must not lose heart.

Sunday morning is still the time when we are most likely to see most of the church gather. There may be limitations with the form we follow and the time we have, but we have an opportunity to invest in that time and allow it to shape our understanding of what it means to be a disciple. Because, regardless of our tradition, I believe that our experience of worshipping together shapes us as disciples. My friends were right; we were different. They just didn't realize the extent of that difference. Far beyond the way we dressed on Sundays, we were being led into a different story of the world, the future and our part in it all.

Whatever our tradition, I want to explore the possibilities offered by two of the most common aspects in our gathered worship. We have a regular form of worship liturgy and we have some form of preaching. This chapter will explore how these aspects of the 'first day of the week' can shape us as whole-life disciples.

But first, let us turn to the expectations we bring to our gatherings.

Sunday expectations

Loosely speaking, I think most of our Sunday gatherings could be typified as being primarily either encounter-centred or education-centred. In the encounter-centred gatherings, people come expecting to meet with God. This could be in the context of charismatic worship or through the Eucharistic liturgy, but a central prayer will be the call for the Spirit to come. It is an emphasis that is experiential.

In the education-centred gatherings, people will come with notebooks primarily expecting to learn something. Encounter-churches spend a lot of time praying or singing, with their eyes closed. Education-churches spend a lot of time listening, with their eyes open.

There are strengths in both traditions, but each one faces specific temptations and challenges.

The temptation for encounter-centred gatherings

We live in a time when the 'empathy economy is booming. Facts are out, feelings are in'.[1] It is the way that we are sold new products. We buy the branded goods, whether that be an Apple computer, Chanel perfume or a BMW car, not just because of the assumed superiority of quality, but because we believe the promises advertisers make about how we will feel: contemporary, refined, sophisticated. We may search the internet for factual reviews, but we will be sold the goods emotionally.

In this culture, then, churches that stress the spiritual–emotional elements of encountering Christianity find fertile ground. I am not suggesting that church leaders manipulate emotions. It is just that, in a context where emotional responses can be encouraged, there will be a lot of people who will find this satisfying. At least for a time.

But there are obvious dangers. As Scot McKnight has written, 'Some folks love church, and what they mean by "loving church" is that they love the experience they get when they go to church.'[2]

That experience can include belonging and being loved, but in many contemporary expressions of worship, the mood can easily become dominated by therapeutic-encounter expectations. Flawed and broken as we all are, we find it remarkably easy to make it all about us. We position ourselves as victims and retell the salvation gospel as a rescue story, but only frame it in personal, emotional–psychological terms.

The temptation for education-centred churches

In these churches, whether theologically conservative or progressive, the temptation is that we help one another become better informed, but do not necessarily enable one another to be better formed. The sermon can take on the form of a lecture, the congregation listening to intricate exegesis of the text or analysis of contemporary society. The assumption is that the profound implications of the biblical text will be self-evident. The listeners may come to be 'fed', but the danger is that nothing changes as a result of this ministry. At the same time, the leaders of these churches can feel the strain of the inflated expectations of their listeners as week by week they look for in-depth insight.

Underlying this approach is the assumption that if we understand more, we will be more likely to change. Our beliefs and understanding are important, but the challenge for many of us is the gap between all we know and what we do. Many of us are wary of placing too many of our expectations on the value of reason. The problem is not solely our disordered thinking, it is our disordered heart.

Clearly there is a need for elements of both these traditions. All encounter without any depth of understanding leads to spiritual flakiness. But emphasis on cognitive understanding without any mystical encounter with the God who is beyond us will result in a dry and cold form of Christianity. Who really wants to live solely in either world?

The search for wisdom and signs for their own sake has always been the temptation for the church. You can see the earliest tensions in Corinth (1 Corinthians 1:22–25; 2:4–59). Wise leaders are aware of the weaknesses of their own traditions and will balance both, but the fundamental danger is that we go to church services for our own needs. Certainly that seemed true of the Corinthians.

Paul kept on emphasizing that they came together for the sake of the other, not for themselves. Whether it was selfishness in eating the shared meal, the complicated situation about head covering and freedom in a context that seemed to suggest strife between men and women or the self-indulgent use of the gift of tongues that alienated others, Paul's acid test for their times of gathered worship was the extent to which others benefited from the activities of the congregation.

If the church can accept the call to be a disciplemaking community, we are right to ask about how our gathered worship practices as a whole can help one another grow as whole-life disciples. We need to ask how our practices can connect with a frontline focus and how they can cumulatively shape one another as disciples of Jesus.

Shaped by our liturgy[3]

Many churches would not use the word 'liturgy' to describe their pattern of worship. They would insist that their church is very 'free' and open to change week by week. In reality, what to an occasional visitor might look like informal spontaneity is, in fact, a fairly standard pathway. A pattern learnt through week-by-week practice.

However, regardless of whether the liturgy is written or simply remembered, the root meaning of the word helps us to see its richness: *leitourgia* is the work of the people. It is our communal focus by the whole community of God's people on God through Scripture, prayer and song that provides a way for us to be reminded that all of life is sacred. It is our responsive act that we offer to God because of who he is. We must always guard against worshipping with an eye on what we can 'get out if it'; we worship because it is our proper response to the revelation of God in Christ.

But we are shaped by our worship practices. The issues that get highlighted in our gatherings together become the touchstone for what is deemed to be most important. If the impression is given that our gathered life is most significant to God, it will be no surprise that our scattered lives as the hurch become overlooked. In fact, it will be at this point of disconnection between the gathered and the scattered experiences that worship becomes distorted. If our everyday, mundane experiences are not included in our gathered worship, then we might enjoy something that is aesthetically beautiful or emotionally moving, but we will have lost the sense of what the Bible would know as true worship.

When the prophets denounced the worship practices of the people of God, it was precisely because they cared deeply about what true worship should involve. They saw that gathered worship could easily get disconnected from the everyday responsibilities that people carried. It became a distinct demonstration of a deep-rooted sacred–secular divided view of life as a whole.

God's anger, mediated through Amos (5:21–27), is still directed towards worshippers who are:

> comfortable in the sanctuary and uncaring in the street.
> Passionate with the congregation in singing hymns,
> indifferent to the poor in their struggle for food. Caught
> up in mystical spirituality in worship but we leave God
> there as we go to work. Amos expects integral worship,
> an authentic connection between the sanctuary and the
> courtroom, worship centre and marketplace, church and
> society.[4]

Amos-approved worship is worship that challenges and enables us to live our whole lives as disciples of Jesus.

The missing dimension

Worshipping together gives us an opportunity to be reminded that our distinctiveness as disciples lies in our understanding of who God is and who we are in relation to him. It's in worship that we have the chance to be re-created week by week as we are made aware of the bigger story of God's salvation. This can change how we see our whole lives:

> We hear all kinds of competing stories when out in our
> scattered lives – stories which focus around selfish ambition,
> faithless worry and godless striving. The symbols, words

and sounds of gathered worship give us an opportunity
to refocus on the radically alternative story of God: the
God of self-sacrifice, who cares about the whole earth, and
sends us out to play our part in his re-creation.[5]

As a leader, in my church, I am worshipping alongside
people working in so many disparate places, Monday to
Saturday.

There's the media technician, working away from home
most weeks, a little lonely and a little disconnected from the
events he is employed for and yet absolutely vital to them. As
we worship together, I am conscious of him trying to balance
all the responsibilities he has, working out what wisdom looks
like for him, and what faithfulness to Christ and work
looks like.

There's the manager of the children's football team, acutely
aware of the texts that are coming in from anxious parents
wondering whether the game will still happen on a very wet
Sunday afternoon. He worships as he prepares to meet the
parents with their mixture of support and criticism as he
settles the petty arguments of the children.

There's the bookkeeper dealing with local businesses that
are trying hard to avoid tax demands. She's worshipping and
wanting to know how to stay righteous in the middle of the
moral dilemmas that others give her.

There's the teacher, so encouraged because three of her
Year 11, bottom-set English class came to tell her that, finally,
they are beginning to understand the book that they are
studying in her class.

There's the actress, worried about whether or not work
will come in this month, but still wondering if she has a
'proper' job, or at least one that is valuable in God's eyes.

And so it goes.

It is too easy to forget these sorts of contexts. It is easier to lead people in acts of worship that solely highlight God's power in creation and his saving power through the cross than it is to find songs, images and words that relate these two central actions of God to our ordinary lives. But if we do not link creation and salvation with our contexts, we have a missing dimension in our worship.[6] If we do not link creation and salvation with our contexts, we have an escapist spirituality.

Our worship needs to widen our imaginations. All those people sitting alongside one another in church, from the technician to the actress, need their imaginations to be continually reshaped by the central truths of the Christian story. These will include the narrative truths of how God has worked in history, as well as the doctrinal truths that explore how salvation, holiness, sin, humanity and everything else provide a framework for seeing the world differently. The truths will include the relationships between answered prayer and the seeming silence of God; the tension of hope and lament.

In other words, our worship together can help us to continually develop a different perspective on our different situations. It's not about just offering one another advice; it's about us getting a bigger picture of the God who loves his own creation so very much. It's about a washed and reshaped imagination.

This is what is possible.

We gather on one day of the week after being the scattered people of God all week. We come with stories to tell of where we have been aware of God acting, of concerns for people and situations that we want to share with the family of God and the need for a renewed earthing in the big story of God's acts of salvation. The answer to the prayer, 'Come, Holy

Spirit', is not simply that our worship offering will be more enlivened, it is that the people of God can re-enter their scattered contexts with a renewed sense of resilience, creativity and boldness. It may be too much to expect our church buildings to be shaken week by week, but is it too daring a prayer that we might see God 'stretch out his hand' in our offices, schools, hospitals and factories week by week? (Acts 4:30–31).

The answer to our prayer that we will learn something is not simply that we are clearer on some doctrinal point or historical accuracy, but that we have been given wisdom to see our situations in a new way. For every glorious miracle that seems to have happened without any human input, there are hundreds of occasions when God transforms the world through the actions of his people and creates something completely new. Those actions will have been shaped by the almost unnoticed accumulation of godly wisdom over time. Indeed, for those caught up in responding creatively to the challenges of their own world, their actions may just have seemed like common sense.

Linking the gathered and the scattered

There are various ways in which we can make the link between the gathered and scattered expressions of church,[7] but two of the key hinge points are how services begin and end.

The opening words contain all sorts of hidden messages. In some cases, we can give the impression that we have come to meet God here, suggesting that our week has been characterized by his absence; or if we give the sense that this is God's house, we unintentionally affirm a spatial sacred–secular divide; or if we encourage people to leave their concerns behind, we can inadvertently suggest that this act of worship will not interact with the 'real world'.

Regardless of style, tradition or resources, the gathering can emphasize three aspects of our engagement with God:

- who we are as the people of God: the missionary people of God who come with stories to tell of where we have seen God at work and are sent back into our worlds as agents of a different kingdom;
- who God the Trinity is as the creator, sustainer and saviour of the whole world: we are co-labourers with God, living out his desires for his own world;
- where we have been embedded in God's world this week: there are particular places that he sends each of us to and we all have a part to play.

These truths will dictate our welcome, our introduction, our opening hymns or songs.

These three truths, then, are reiterated as we leave to love and serve the Lord in the week. Our journey of worship will have encouraged us to have a renewed awareness of the whole story of God and should have offered fresh encouragement to live as the people of God wherever we find ourselves.

There are many more ways that we can help people get a new perspective on their lives, but these two pivotal moments seem to be key in emphasizing our core identity as the missionary people of God, living out our lives of worship wherever we find ourselves.

If all this is clear in the minds of those who lead worship, then other aspects of our gatherings will flow naturally to include a whole-life perspective. So, for example, when we think of the intercessory prayer that happens as part of our

services, it becomes easier to see how we might include
Monday-to-Saturday issues here.

SOMETIMES IT LOOKS LIKE THIS

*Shannon is the minister in a small, rural Irish Methodist church.
Those who worship there know one another really well, but
struggle to be open with one other in church about the things that
particularly concern them. They display a rugged resilience, not
unusual in people who have had to dig out a living from fields for
generations.*

*Shannon respects that, but also wanted to encourage them to
be able to support one another more specifically and be able to
connect their worship with their Monday-to-Saturday experiences.
This is what she did:*

*'At the end of August, I felt a great need to personalize our
Sunday morning prayers, but also recognize the need for
confidentiality. I shared that with my folks and they seemed
willing to give it a go. I started passing round a page for people
to write their prayer concerns and I use that page during
intercessory prayer. This has given me a better understanding of
what is in their hearts and minds and it has been an entry point
for further conversations that have been initiated by the people.'*

It's a simple way to connect their prayer with their lives.

We don't need to change our worship patterns so much as
ensure that our worship practices fully reflect all that it means
to be a whole-life disciple.

Remember the life-giver

The danger in trying to connect the aspects of Sunday worship
with people's frontline experiences is that it can become

mechanistic. At the heart of our worship, our encounters as well as our formation are the result of the deep work of the Spirit. In Ephesians, Paul urges the believers to be filled with the Spirit (5:18), which is followed by the call to sing to one another. The outflow of the presence of the Spirit is the songs that will encourage those around us. But this is not an escape from the reality that the Ephesian believers would have experienced. The encouragement comes in the midst of the reminders that they were called to be light in the dark world, to live and act differently among their neighbours and to have distinctive marriage, family and work relationships (4:17 – 6:9).

The work of the Spirit is not to insulate us from the challenges of everyday life, but to offer life in the midst of all that happens around us. Without this reality, we will only be left with the empty mechanics of church life. But when the Spirit enlivens all that we have, new things can come alive. We become churches where 'Theology comes alive in conversation and prayer, in worship and community'.[8]

IN PRACTICE
Worship practices that engage the frontline

Using relevant images
If you use projected images as a background to words of songs displayed on a screen, what images are chosen? If all your images are of countryside, sunsets and gorgeous views that include no humans, it is likely that worshippers will imagine these are the places where you are most likely to encounter God. These settings may provide welcome respite to busy people, but most of us spend our lives surrounded by people, in the shadows of buildings flanked by busy traffic. Would these images help us to have a greater sense of God's glory in the reality of most of our Monday-to-Saturday lives?

Who is prayed for in your services?

In some churches, the only way you get mentioned in prayer is if you are unable to be there: either because you are too ill or you're overseas on some mission. Find reasons to pray for people who are part of the congregation and facing joys and challenges on their own frontlines. Here are some examples of the kinds of things you could do.

- Commission people for new posts in voluntary groups or new responsibilities in the workplace.
- Use the special days and seasons in the calendar as points that encourage missional living. Mothers'/Fathers' days offer the opportunity to pray for parents as disciples who are seeking to disciple their own families; September is a time to pray for all those involved in education, from children to adults; autumn harvest services give us the chance to reflect on the way we provide for ourselves and others through work.
- Use all-age services to the full. These gatherings, where children and adults worship together in a more relaxed format, offer the easiest opportunities for people to share their frontline experiences with one another. They also provide chances to explore the joys and challenges of being a Christian in those places. For example, if your all-age gatherings include some element of craft activity, it's not hard to get people to draw the places where they spend much of their time or to create modelling clay models of the people they know on their frontlines or to draw maps of the journeys they take to get to schools, workplaces, clubs and groups.What could be better than having adults and children gathered around tables together, talking to one another about the things that bring them joy in their Monday-to-Saturday lives and the things they struggle with?

What could be better than going to work knowing that in
your wallet is a handwritten prayer for you, on a card given
to you by a ten-year-old, who listened to you explain a little
more about your life and wrote a prayer for you?

See Sam and Sara Hargreaves' book, *Whole Life Worship*, and the
accompanying resources that can be found on the LICC's website
for more ideas.[9]

5. PREACHING THAT EQUIPS US FOR THE FRONTLINE

I was so warm.

The room was heaving with people. More than usual. Lots of strangers. Men with different accents, from places that I'd heard of but never visited. Men with stories to tell.

It had been a long day. I'd been up at dawn, as usual, collecting the water, carrying the washing away, buying the wine, cleaning the house and paying the money we owed for meat and fish.

I wouldn't have missed going out again that night, though. It was the first day of the week. Our day. One of the highlights of my week. I met friends along the road and was glad to be welcomed into the big house we were meeting in again. We sat at the table and were served bread, meat and wine. Such a luxury after a week of fetching and carrying for others.

After a while, one of the visitors called for our attention and, after he had prayed, we sang a hymn while we passed the bread to one another and drank the local wine. It was that moment in the week when it all came together again, when everything made sense, when the past and the present coincided.

*When everything was cleared away, we all tried to get a place to
listen to him. Children were squirming on the knees of their mothers,
some of the men stood, while others sat where they could. I'd been
smart, though. The room was getting warmer and I knew that if I
could haul myself up to the window, I'd get the fresh air. If it got a
bit boring, I could look out towards the theatre and the running
track.*

*I wasn't bored, but I was tired and I could feel myself drifting
away.*

*I don't know what happened next, but suddenly I was on the
ground outside and everyone was around me. Lots of anxious faces.
Not least my master. He looked particularly anxious. It was only
later that they told me I'd fallen and the visitor had hugged me and
prayed. Only then had my eyes opened.*

*We went back upstairs, had something else to eat and carried on
listening to the visitor, Paul, preach. To be honest, I was sitting there
just feeling completely confused.*

*That was twenty years ago and now I am one of the church elders.
Sometimes when I'm just about to preach, people remind me not to
take too long. After all, I know the dangers of falling asleep in church.*

*But I also know how it feels to come back to life when a preacher
prays for you.*

If anyone might have had good reason to suggest that Sunday
gatherings with hymns, prayers and preaching didn't work, it
would be Eutychus. He wouldn't be the last Christian to use
the time offered by the preacher as time to follow his own
track of thought, reading the next passage in the Bible or just
floating in mental free fall, aware of all that is to be done in
the following week. He wouldn't be the last Christian to find
that he had fallen asleep.

People still sleep through sermons, tired after a long week.
They just tend not to sit next to open windows.

This may be an uncomfortable truth, at least to preachers, but, two thousand years on, fundamentally, we share the same practices that fed the earliest church in their disciple-making activities. That includes preaching: the time when one person, who has made time to explore the biblical text ahead of the congregation, tries to engage everyone, distant from the text in time and place, with the ground-shaking possibilities contained within it.

Preaching that connects with the frontline[1]

Preaching is one of the main ways in which leaders can equip people for their frontline over a long period of time. It happens as preachers explicitly make the links between passages from the Bible and the situations that members of the congregation are facing in their frontline contexts.

But this must be more than an occasional gesture – a short series on 'work' every two years, for example. For those who are currently in paid employment or want to be in employment or who have been employed in the past, they know that 'work' is not one topic among many; it is their permanent context.

The workplace offers a sense of worth as well as times of stress. It's the place where friendships are formed. For some, they come to identify themselves so closely with their work that they either take great pride in what they do or feel slightly ashamed to admit that this is what they have to give their time to each day.

So, equipping people for the particular frontline of their workplaces cannot be limited to an occasional gesture. It's about a certain type of posture on the part of the preacher. Gestures are fine and are appreciated when offered, but a posture is permanent. A gesture happens when there's a situation that seems to require something particular, but a posture has grown over time and affects the way everything is seen.

Congregations need preachers who have a posture shaped by the awareness of where people spend most of their time, wherever that may be. They need preachers who believe that, as people are discipled by a growing understanding of the gospel, they will live confidently as representatives of a different kingdom in these workplaces.

Sermons on equipping are not just about delivering particular information; they are the fruit of preachers who have developed their own equipping posture. It is seen in the way they draw on the texts from the Bible and the way they approach their own congregation.

Approaching the Bible

We come to the Bible believing that God has the intention of using the text to shape our thinking and our actions. But, despite that, because of the challenges of living as a Christian in secularized society, it is tempting to believe that, while certain things may be true for church life or personal lives, in the 'real world', we have to live according to a different set of rules. Faith can be deemed to be relevant to the private spaces of life, but have nothing to offer practically in public life.

The Bible offers no support for this domestication of faith. Most actions in the Bible take place in the public arena of challenging workplaces: Joseph in Egypt, Ruth and Boaz navigating an unlikely relationship in the context of a farm, Daniel in the Babylonian civil service, Philemon dealing with a rebellious member of his household in Colosse and so on. There are many such passages in the Bible; more than might be appreciated at first glance.

Most of the prophetic oracles concern themselves with the political issues of the day. The decisions made by national

leaders about national security (for example, Isaiah 31) and by
local landowners about the development of land (for example,
Isaiah 5:8–10) concerned the prophets because they revealed
the poverty of the spiritual life of the country (for example,
Isaiah 5).

Much of the wisdom teaching is about a spirituality that is
earthed in the daily decisions concerning money, property,
loyalty and competition (for example, Proverbs 10–11).

Most of the poetic literature delights in using the settings
of everyday life to help people engage with the whole-life
God. On some occasions, everyday life will reflect the way
David believed God had helped him as a soldier (for example,
Psalm 18). On other occasions, he will use the peaceful image
of toddlers at ease in their mother's arms to explain the peace
he feels before his God (for example, Psalm 131).[2]

The writers didn't use these situations as mere examples, in
the way some preachers might use recent events in the news.
Their lives of faith were lived out self-consciously in these
public arenas. It would have been baffling for them to think
that faith in God would not engage with the whole of life.

But that didn't mean it was easy to keep on believing or
living faithfully. There rarely was a golden era in the Old
Testament when it was a simple thing to follow God. It was
very difficult for the Israelites living under oppressive regimes
in Egypt to remain faithful to him. It was equally challenging
for the exiled worshippers far away from their own land
dreaming of home. Even when the people of God were in
their own country, their lives were dominated by the extent
to which their own kings were faithful to God.

Nor is it the case that the New Testament held out any
more attractive propositions for the early Christians. Early
disciples were always more likely to be shaped by the
prevailing culture than they were by the teaching of Jesus;

that's why the teaching in the epistles kept reminding them of the cross and how their relationships were to be shaped by this understanding of Jesus. Yet, when they were shaped in this way, they faced the real prospect of being persecuted for their faith. It has never been easy.

This is worth remembering when we are guiding people to enter the biblical story. We are preaching to some people who may feel that their world is increasingly hostile to the Christian faith. With others, we are trying to remind them of their central identity as children of God, even as they live in a culture that offers the prospect of numerous false identities. This should not result in the wringing of hands, however; it has always been like this.

Recognizing that this was the situation for the earliest readers of epistles and gospels had the greatest impact on my own preaching. It meant that I could place my church in line with these early Christians. Together we were re-entering the world where the prayers of the early Christians were shouted out in exuberant praise and disappointed lament. We were re-entering the world where saints, neither now nor then, are ever as good as they wished they were, but were caught up into God's purposes all the same. We were re-entering the world where the traces of God have been marked out for us, in order that we can work alongside him in our own world.

This is our primary task for those who have the privilege of preaching in gathered worship. The task is not to give a series of tips for people struggling with the world around them. Rather, we need to remind one another about the nature of the world in which we live and help to discern where God might be.

But it is not enough to be convinced of the biblical contexts. We need to be aware of the contexts that are faced by the congregation.

Approaching the congregation

The major difference between a preacher who has deep roots in a local worshipping community and a general biblical commentator is that the preacher has the chance to know those who are listening to the sermon. The commentary may help you get to know the text really well; the preacher can know the congregation really well. The commentary explores the full range of the text, its implications for doctrine and the horizons of potential meaning. The preacher is self-consciously self-limiting. The preacher is not seeking to say everything about the text, but is opening up the aspects of the text that will be of most help and encouragement to these disciples of Jesus at this time because of the situations that they are facing or will face.

Immediately someone will want to say, 'But you can't do that for everyone.' Of course, that is true. The teenager's context self-evidently differs from that of the retired widower. However, there are some things we can do to ensure that we increase our chances of connecting with those to whom we preach.

SOMETIMES IT LOOKS LIKE THIS

Philip is really aware of this challenge and tries to meet it head on. At the beginning of the week, he will meet someone in his congregation for a conversation about the text that will be the foundation for the preaching at the weekend. He asks them to share their responses to the text. He invites different people each time: people of different ages, ethnicities and social backgrounds. At that point he is primarily listening. Then, on Thursday, he will meet with someone different and, over coffee, let that person know what he is preaching and how he feels it connects with everyday life. His intention is to test his intuition, but also to listen for the connection that the person in front of him would make.

You might feel that Philip's is an impossible schedule. Yet, for this preacher, he simply sees it as a fundamental part of his preparation. For him, it is no stranger than trawling through the commentaries looking for meaning or spending hours on YouTube looking for a brilliant video that would illustrate all he wanted to say.

What is clear is that this process has a significant effect on how the sermon is preached. Contrast it with what happens to the vast majority of preachers. They might be clear on the text that will be preached at the beginning of the week and, alongside the private work of reading, praying and reflecting, there are visits to be made to sick people or those who are spiritually drifting. There are church leadership meetings where the present situation of the church is reviewed and a different future is dreamt of and planned for. Those of us who preach regularly readily recognize the influence that conversations have on our preaching, albeit subconsciously.

Put simply, if we spend all our time with those who are in need or those who share the responsibility for the church, the connections we will instinctively make in preaching will either be ones that emphasize the care God has for us or the future God has for us as a church community. Both are important aspects of life as Christians, but there is more. There are those who listen, for whom life is fairly normal. They do have the common frustrations, challenges and disappointments, but primarily they are listening for something that connects their everyday world with the world of the Bible.

Questions that help

There is a set of questions that I have found helpful as I am preparing sermons. They are not the traditional, helpful questions connected with exegesis and exposition. Those

disciplines still need to happen. These additional questions
help me to keep a wider view on how this text will help us as
a community grow as disciples.

1. **What does the text reveal about Jesus or God or,
   more widely, the gospel?**
   This question stops me racing to find the 'relevance'
   too soon. Sometimes this desire to help people see
   how central the Bible can be to their daily lives can,
   unintentionally, make it appear that the Bible is essentially
   about us. The Bible is not essentially about us – it's about
   God's salvation purposes worked out for the whole of
   the creation. We get wrapped up into that story but,
   primarily, we read the Bible in order to know this God,
   rather than merely to find tips for living or comfort for
   difficult days. This is a massive help as we seek to
   encourage one another to live faithfully for Christ. God
   does have a plan, not just for our lives, but for his world.
   He does act in surprising, miraculous ways and yet at
   other times he seems strangely absent. This is the God we
   want to encounter. This is the God we need to worship.
   This is the God in whose hands we place our lives.

2. **How does this text shape our understanding of what
   it means to be a disciple?**
   Primarily, preaching is part of the disciplemaking task.
   If, as a church community, we understand that together
   we are learning what it means to be a disciple, then we
   will be alert to the Bible's teaching and the ways in
   which it encourages us to live counterculturally. As
   a preacher, I am less interested in people having a full
   grasp of all the disagreements that the text might have
   provoked over the years than I am in seeing how this
   text will continue to shape us as disciples of Jesus.

3. **How does this text connect with conversations I have been part of recently?**
A preacher needs to be a good listener. It's more than being a sensitive listener; it's about being able to take seriously what you are hearing. Often people will share all sorts of information about the joys and challenges of their lives. Good preachers will recall these conversations as they prepare their sermons. These insights into ordinary life provide the connections for the preacher, the text and this congregation at this moment.

4. **What does this passage lead us to pray?**
Somehow the sermon needs to inspire us to believe that more is possible on our frontlines than we might have otherwise imagined. For that to be the case, we will be pulled into prayer because the challenge will be too great for us alone.

5. **What does this passage require us to do?**
This is the final test for a sermon. This is the difference between an interesting lecture and a sermon that shapes our living. It helps to keep the sermon practical, rather than staying in the realm of the personal and private. It keeps the preacher earthed rather than abstract. Of course, the 'doing' might be worship or offering prayers of wonder or it might involve apologizing to a friend or ensuring that you are the first to offer to buy the next round of drinks when out with colleagues.

SOMETIMES IT LOOKS LIKE THIS

The joy of the Bible for me is that I can return to familiar passages and then be stunned to find a new perspective that had eluded me up to that point.

Reading Luke's account of the Lord's Prayer is such an example. It is so familiar that it is easy for our eyes to skim down the page, especially if at some time in the past you have underlined the promises: 'Ask and it will be given to you; seek and you will find; knock and the door will be opened to you' (Luke 11:10).

Kenneth Bailey's works[3] have alerted many of us to the significance of Middle Eastern culture and how a basic awareness of it can open up the New Testament in new ways. Reflecting on the parable that follows the prayer, it's important to note what is going on.

One man goes to a friend because other friends have arrived and, unreasonably given the time of night, expect to be fed. If they are sent to their lodging without food, the host will be shamed. Understanding this cultural imperative unlocks the impact of the passage: 'The host **must** serve his guest and the guest **must** eat.'[4]

But the host has no bread.

What will the host do?

It's brilliant. He makes it someone else's problem.

He goes to the window of another friend and, though the man will not get out of bed, because he is a friend, he cannot ignore (a brilliant phrase) the 'shameless audacity' of the shamed host (Luke 11:8).

The promise of asking, seeking and knocking that brings the whole section to a close now sits in a context that the story has set up. You are being asked for things that you cannot reasonably produce, but you can go to the one who does have enough. The one who will answer your requests. The one who will supply what you lack.

It wasn't hard to reflect on the conversations that I had had with the businessman who was about to have a major meeting regarding refinancing his company or the teacher and health workers struggling with the targets they had to meet or the harassed parents of teenagers, and the rest, to make people see how this passage was so vitally relevant to us: that God is not embarrassed by our prayers of shameless audacity. That he will supply what is lacking so that we will have what is needed to offer to others. That there is wisdom to be shared about how to thrive when under these pressures, but also, ultimately, our resource will be found as we call to the one we know has the bread when we have none.

This ancient book comes alive in every generation to everyone in that generation who reads it. Those who preach have the privilege of awakening people to its joys and challenges as we help one another read it through the lenses of our frontline contexts.

IN PRACTICE
Preaching practices that engage the frontline
In preparing sermons, you need to understand the contexts of your listeners. The following suggestions offer you ways to understand fully some of the pressures and opportunities that they face.

- Bring together a number of people who would represent the demography of your congregation and share the ideas you have for a series of sermons, encouraging them to reflect on the ways in which the text would shape their frontline experiences and expectations.
- Invite your leadership team to reflect with you about the things they find helpful in the sermons and listen to what they feel would help more. Try hard not to be defensive.

You might have things you could ask them to do that would help you as a speaker.

- Visit people in their frontline contexts and ask them about how the recent sermons have connected their experience of gathered church with their scattered life. Somehow, being in a frontline context, wherever it may be, offers the chance of a more focused conversation.
- From time to time, distribute cards and ask everyone to write down one topic they would really like to hear about in a sermon or a series of sermons.
- Share sermons where appropriate. For example, one of the regular preachers could plan and deliver the sermon in collaboration with somebody from within the church involved in a specific sector, such as healthcare, mental health or finance. It makes for great, relevant and applied teaching.
- Include three whole-life application questions in the weekly bulletin. For example, if the passage is from Luke 11, you could ask the following kinds of questions.

  1. What unreasonable demands will you face this week?
  2. What part does prayer play in helping you to develop resilience?
  3. What role can you play as a 'friend' to those who are struggling in your workplace?

These questions may provide food for thought and fuel for discussion at the end of the service and during the week.

6. SMALL GROUPS THAT ENCOURAGE US FOR THE FRONTLINE

It had been another frustrating evening after weeks of frustrating evenings. We were together, on the border, ready to enter the province, ready to share the good news, but every time we discussed the various options ahead of us, we just felt that we shouldn't move. At least, not yet. Indeed, we felt that we couldn't. For some of us, this was just a vague feeling, but Silas was adamant. 'Not here, not now', he kept saying, but he never explained why.

I began to wonder just how long this would last. Silas had been right in the past. We trusted that he could be right again. It didn't stop it being difficult, though.

What was God doing?

It had seemed an obvious plan: go north, aim for the Black Sea coast and soon we would have covered the whole area. We'd heard there were small groups of believers living along that coast, people gathered from so many different backgrounds. It was inevitable that we would find people interested in all that we were sharing. People who've travelled tend to be open-minded – they've seen so much and heard so many tales, they aren't afraid of foreigners. We were sure that it was the right thing to do.

But sitting in the town square, just a short distance from the border, we were confused and frustrated. It was hard to work out what was happening. We knew the way to the coast, the road was well made and clearly marked. We prayed together, a prayer that was part confusion, part frustration, and we knew our plans were not going to be as we had imagined.

Really early the next morning, Paul came bounding into the room. 'I know what we should do, we need to go west.' He had done this sort of thing before, but this was different. He spoke of a dream of a man who was calling to us to come to his people.

We got dressed and began to pray together. As we did, things began to fall into place; we sensed that this was right. He was impetuous and sometimes he did say things that he would regret later, but I'd grown to trust him. When I first met him, he intimidated me, but over the years, I'd come to appreciate his many gifts.

I changed because I'd been with him and I think he changed as well, because of us.

The world suddenly became so much bigger for us than it had been. I don't think any of us on our own would have had the courage to go.

But together, it was a different matter.

At first sight, reflecting on the experience of Paul and his companions and their confusion in Troas may seem a long way from our experience of small groups in church. They were a group with a sense of a mission to engage in. They were a group of people from mixed backgrounds. They were able to share their lives together. Many small groups that we experience can seem very tame in comparison.

But they can be a significant part of a disciplemaking church. As Walton suggests, the very act of joining a small group can be a sign of our intention to grow as disciples:

> By our willingness to join and participate in small groups
> we signal our desire to walk with others on the road to
> transformation. Recognising that God forms us through
> various means in mission, worship and community, joining
> a small group for a task, for study, personal support or
> missionary endeavour is a symbolic commitment to being
> disciples together, living with diversity and open to the growth
> that may come to us from others – for the sake of the
> kingdom and our transformation within it.[1]

In the light of these rich possibilities of helping one another
live 'for the sake of the kingdom' and the potential to be
transformed, why do more people not join such a group?

Most of us know that we need others around us to help
us grow. Most of us know that we need people who know us
over time in such a way that they will keep us on track as
disciples of Jesus. Most of us know that we need to be in relationships with people who are not natural friends, so that we
can have some of our rough edges rubbed off. Most of us
know we need some form of setting that is smaller than our
regular Sunday gathering.

Most people do not belong to such a group. I think I understand why.

Once upon a time, I was part of a football team, but I
couldn't commit to being there every Saturday afternoon.

So I played squash with a friend instead.

Arrangements could be more flexible. My friend understood when I rang to cancel.

Then he got too old to play.

So now I run.

Alone.

Sometimes.

It's hard when there's so much to do.

Here's the thing: I enjoy all these activities and they do me
good. It's just that time, responsibilities and other commitments beat me most weeks. It's a common story. The realities
of my week defeat the intentions of the things that I enjoy
and do me good.

You can try to help me by insisting that I need to do these
things. You can make me feel guilty about not being able to
say 'no'. You can send me a magic app that will organize my
life. But I fear I know what the outcome will be.

Time, responsibilities and other commitments defeat our
best intentions and our best desires. We may think it, but this
is not a problem unique to the twenty-first century. The writer
to the Hebrews was equally dismayed by Christians who were
losing their appetite to meet together:

> Let us hold unswervingly to the hope we profess, for he
> who promised is faithful. And let us consider how we may
> spur one another on towards love and good deeds, not giving
> up meeting together, as some are in the habit of doing, but
> encouraging one another – and all the more as you see the
> Day approaching.
> (Hebrews 10:23–25)

The writer had a clear idea of what help these early Christians
could give one another to achieve something: love and good
deeds. These small groups of Christians who came together
would help to shape one another's actions in their everyday
lives.

Although it's unusual for churches to have more than about
a third of their worshippers as regular small group attendees,
they are a significant asset to any church that wants to take
seriously the need to support one another's lives on their
frontlines. They are worth investing in.

Developing confidence in the value of groups

A few years ago, Roger Walton, a Methodist leader in the UK, did some research into the benefit of small groups for those who attended them. His research was conducted in 'ordinary' churches of different sizes and locations. His findings were really encouraging. The results of attending small groups in their churches were that:

- 77 per cent of people reported that they were more confident in their faith;
- 76 per cent were more able to connect their faith and everyday life;
- 72 per cent were more accepting and forgiving of others;
- 79 per cent said that it had strengthened their prayer life;
- 68 per cent said that it had given them more confidence in speaking about their faith to others;
- 87 per cent said that the group had brought them closer to God.[2]

These figures are probably higher than any of us could have expected. We may wonder if the people surveyed were more generous at that moment than they may have felt on a cold wet November evening. We may wonder if they felt that they should have given the 'right answers' to the questions.

Surveys sometimes don't tell the whole story, but maybe the respondents here were telling the truth about their experiences of ordinary home groups in ordinary UK churches.

When I read the results, it led me to wonder whether sometimes we have sold the experience of small groups short.

In conversation, leaders will often suggest that their big hope is that people will be formed as disciples through the church small groups system. However, when you listen to the way that small groups are promoted in most churches, you would not come to that conclusion. At regular intervals, a congregation will be urged to join small groups because that is where friendships can be made in a growing church where it is easy to feel anonymous. Alternatively, people may be told that the groups are the means by which pastoral care can be offered. Friendship and care become the two public offerings when, behind the scenes, the hope was for discipling relationships.

This is where Walton's findings need to be tempered by his wider research. Alongside the almost staggeringly positive feedback of small group members reported above was the sober reality that 'an analysis of the responses suggested that what people value most are the relational dynamics of the small group and the sense of pastoral support they offer.'[3] These small groups succeeded in providing a safe space for deep friendships to grow. However, when asked what words would express what they most appreciated about belonging to a group, 'the words "mission", "outreach", "evangelism", "serving" and "neighbours" were not mentioned by anyone.'[4] Although people may have recorded an increased confidence in speaking about the gospel and connecting faith and life, 'There is little evidence that the group experience pushes them to engage or seek God in the more complex and contested areas of human society.'[5]

If we know that small groups can be the place where strangers become deep friends and changes do happen, however, is it impossible to believe that these relationships can be the support for intentional frontline living? The reason that those surveyed never mentioned how the groups had supported their mission, nor engaged in the more complex situations of Christian living, may simply have been that they did not think that was what small groups were supposed to do. They may well have believed that they were all about pastoral support and relationships.

What would happen if we used the suggested outcomes from research like this and were confident enough to say, 'If you want to know how to connect your faith with your everyday life, we have found that at least three-quarters of people who attend small groups say that those groups will help you to do this.' For that to happen, groups will need to develop conversations that count and relationships that challenge.

Conversations that count

For years, I was part of a men's prayer group. We tried to keep one another faithful to Jesus in our everyday lives by asking one another the most basic of questions: 'What's happening?'

We would take as long as we needed. Sometimes the answer would be 'not much' and we would move to the next person, who might have taken the rest of the evening. One day it is was my turn to take the time.

> At that time I was commuting to work, a 100-mile return journey each day, up and down the motorway that doubles up as a car park much of the time – the M6. Not the easiest of journeys. After a particularly trying day, I'd arrived home with 30 minutes to spare before the men's group was due to begin. It meant there was just enough time to explore a regular concern with my teenage children about why their breakfast bowls were still lying in the same place in the lounge as this morning, now that it was dark outside. We had a 'conversation' about whose bowls they were.

I was left mystified because it turned out they didn't belong to anybody!

I went into the kitchen where my wife asked me to relax and stop nagging, wondering why I had come back in such a bad mood. Again. We had a 'conversation' about that.

The cat got between my legs.

I shouted at the cat.

I left in a flurry of self-righteousness for the men's group where I retold all that had happened. I was looking for a sympathetic hearing.

They didn't let me down. As I came to the end of my rant, they looked at me and then one man said, 'Yes, that M6, it's a real pain, isn't it?!'

As I got ready to go to bed that night, I reflected on all that had happened. I realized that we had such a strong sense of disclosure in the group that I could have finished the story by telling them anything and they would have sympathized and prayed for my journey.

The group's reaction was everything I wanted and nothing I needed.

What I needed wasn't understanding, what I needed was someone to ask me how I was going to handle the stresses of leadership at work differently; how I was going to deal with my family in a way that meant they didn't just get the overspill of my frustration; how I was going to stay married or, at least, how I was going to stay married to a wife who wouldn't regret being married to me.

I knew then that we had a situation. We had a great group in which to share problems. We did not have a group that could disciple one another for our frontlines.

I believe the same could be said of many groups in many churches.

We need small groups if we are going to grow as disciples. But they have to be groups that have a clear intentionality.

Relationships that challenge

The assumption I have made about the relationships that develop in most small groups is they will be different from natural friendships. Friendships have a crucial role to play in our formation, and we will explore them in the next chapter, but it is important to be open about the fact that small groups may not provide the friendships many hope for.

They do not need to.

In some cases, they are unlikely to.

In fact, one of the benefits of choosing to build relationships in a small group with people you have little in common with is precisely because of what can emerge from doing this.

If we recognize that we belong to a church in order to be formed as disciples of Jesus and schooled in the ways of Jesus, then we will learn to value people who are different from us. We will listen closely to those who see things differently from the way we do. We will offer support to others who are in contexts that we cannot easily imagine. We will learn how to practise the fruit of the Spirit: love, joy, peace, patience, kindness, goodness, faithfulness, gentleness and self-control.

If we are to be shaped by our experience of small groups, then we need to accept some foundational truths that will reflect the experience of the earliest disciples of Jesus. The first of which is perhaps the most mind-blowing. When we gather, Jesus is among us. In the passage loved by organizers of poorly attended prayer meetings, Jesus promised that where two or three people get together 'in his name', he will turn up as well (Matthew 18:20). As France so aptly puts it,

'That gives a whole new dimension to an apparently insignificant gathering of two or three concerned disciples.'[6]

This promise is in the context of turmoil and disagreement. The assumption that Jesus makes about his new kingdom community is that there will be conflict, people will hurt one another, we will sin and this sin will affect others. We will need to learn how to forgive, to an absurd degree (Matthew 18:22), and we will have to make difficult decisions regarding those who hurt others and refuse to turn away from their actions (Matthew 18:15–17).

This small community offers the prospect of life but, for that to happen, Jesus expects it to be an honest community. It will help us to face up to the darkest parts of our characters. It will allow us to be known by others as we really are and it will be a context in which we can be honest about our whole lives. It's a circle of people to whom we can make ourselves mutually accountable, not merely for the way we treat one another but also for the way we live our scattered lives when we are away from the group. It's a high call, but Christians in every generation have known that this is what it takes to grow.

SOMETIMES IT LOOKS LIKE THIS

Like many Bible colleges, the one I used to teach in had an infrastructure of small pastoral groups that students were assigned to in their first year and continued in until they left in their third and final year. Taking out the long holiday periods, they didn't actually spend much time together, though the time they did have was often very intense.

As a tutor, I was always interested to see the groups develop over the years. In the first term of the first year, many of the groups' members were excited, keen and eager to experience this new life, seemingly appreciative of one another. By the first term of the second year, there was little novelty left in the college experience; they had coped with the highs and lows of assignments being graded and they began to find one another irritating. In the small groups of twelve, you could see the subgroups emerge and the outsiders being isolated. The reasons for people being outsiders could be very varied. It could have been because of their age, not being at the same stage of life as the majority. It could have been that they held different theological views from the rest and were not afraid to air them. It could just have been that they found groups difficult. There was no doubt that it was often a disorientating time for them. Their biggest challenge was that they had to keep attending. It was mandatory.

By the beginning of the third year, something would change. Somehow, in ways that would have been difficult to document, the outsiders were accepted and, more than that, valued and, in some cases, protected. This was the greatest gift that the groups gave people. They made us kinder and more fully human towards one another.

What it took was the discipline of time and stability.

It takes time to learn to be discomforted by others.

It takes time to realize that we don't all see the world the same way.

It takes time to listen.

It takes time to understand.

It takes time to be aware of the presence of Jesus among us.

It also takes stability. The students couldn't leave, even when they wanted to. That discipline of stability yielded its own fruit. Maybe in too many places we leave too soon. Persuaded that we don't fit, and made to feel that we don't belong, we leave. We then miss being the gift that the group so desperately needs – the gift of being different, the gift that produces growth.

There is no easy solution to the problem of encouraging time-poor people to make long-term commitments to small groups. But the least we can do is demonstrate how valuable the result of this commitment is and can be by belonging to a group ourselves.

Why this mattered in Rome[7]

This way of seeing one another, and helping one another grow, matters not because we want to have great small groups in our churches. It matters because it is one of the ways that we will be formed into a very different type of people in our cultural context. And that is of essential significance when we are thinking about how disciples can be nurtured so that they live distinctive lives on their frontlines.

When Paul was introducing himself to the church in Rome, he took time to retell the grand story of creation to consummation before turning to outlining his understanding of what it meant to live as a disciple of Jesus in first-century Rome.

But before he tackled the responsibilities of being a citizen of Rome, he painted a picture of how belonging to the Christian community would shape people to act counter-culturally.

Chapter 12 begins with him urging people to offer their 'everyday, ordinary life – your sleeping, eating, going-to-work, and walking-around life – and place it before God as an offering' (Romans 12:1, MSG).

Then, at first sight, he seems to outline a random collection of encouragements to the church. It is easy for us to dismiss them as being obvious as our eye skates down the page. But, if we stop and realize how countercultural they are, then maybe we too will be challenged by the prospect of how belonging to this body of Christians can shape us for the whole of life.

He begins by saying, 'Do not think of yourself more highly than you ought' (Romans 12:3). In a firmly demarcated hierarchical society, this was threatening. To be a male free-born Roman citizen gave you the right to think of yourself as being on the top rung of society's ladder. It gave you access to education, wealth and power. Paul's talk of the distribution of gifts being provided by God to the church, not on the basis of Roman society's understanding of significance, but on the wider basis of faith, was subversive. It may not be too fanciful to wonder what would have happened if the community recognized that one of the household slaves had been given a gift of teaching. Would the householder have sat meekly, ready to be taught? If he had, what would his pagan neighbours have thought when they heard what had happened?[8]

When Paul urges the church to be 'devoted to one another in love' (Romans 12:10), he is suggesting a completely different way of seeing one another. Relationships have less to do with rank or wealth or status and everything to do with seeing one another as brothers or sisters in Christ.

If some of this was challenging for the free-born, it would have confronted the slaves equally as their responses would have put their own futures in jeopardy. If they were to 'share with the Lord's people who are in need' (Romans 12:13) by using their own savings, the day when they might be able to buy their own freedom would have receded into the distance.

But this new community ethic would spill out into radically different responses in their scattered lives. They would bless those who persecuted them, they would be willing to associate themselves with people from across the social strata without any sense of embarrassment and they would not seek revenge, but allow wrongs to be done to them. They would be different – radically different (Romans 12:14–21).

Where would they have learnt this way? In their gatherings as they came together to pray and encourage one another.

The question is whether or not our experiences in small groups can be similarly formative. Do our small groups lead us to act radically differently from the rest of our culture? How can our experience of close relationships in small groups shape people for their frontline contexts?

Why this matters now

Any church, at heart, has the potential to be a gathering of those who are both dissimilar to one another as well as totally committed to one another. Small groups are not the easiest aspect of church life to keep focused on, but the possibilities that they provide are worth the energy that they take.

However, groups can stray from achieving their full potential. The leaders need to be clear as to the purpose of the groups as well as the roles that they need to play. If the groups become contexts in which people share wisdom for the wider situations of life, then people will begin to change. The connection to their whole lives will be very evident. But this is a change of culture for many churches. We have to move from small groups being viewed as the primary places in which to receive pastoral care to places where we will be equipped to live artfully and skilfully as disciples of Jesus on our frontlines.

Characters can be formed when small group leaders and members become alert to the ways in which they can help one another learn new skills. This will be seen in the ways that we listen to one another, talk about and to one another, support one another, seek to understand one another, protect one another, ask for help from one another, offer help to one another, receive from one another and honour one another. If we learn these skills in the context of these gathered relationships, there is a possibility that we will live differently when we scatter throughout the rest of the week.

It can only begin as we learn to act differently with one another in groups where intentional relationships are made, sustained and through which we are gradually changed.

IN PRACTICE
Small group practices that engage with the frontline

Ensure clarity about the group's purpose
We can shape small groups in ways that take seriously our call to be disciples in the frontline contexts of our everyday lives. The groups stop being primarily friendship groups; that level of relationship may or may not develop. They stop being a place to simply share our struggles and can become the equipping places that enable us to see clearly how our faith intersects with the cultures of the places in which we find ourselves in most of the time. They stop being a luxury for the time-rich and become more compelling for the time-poor.

This will mean that there is a shared clarity about the purpose of groups.

Both leaders and members need to share the belief that belonging to these groups will shape their characters, allow them to grow in confidence and enable them to connect faith with their everyday circumstances. If no one is able to explain clearly what the purpose of the groups is, everyone will assign their own understanding instead. It's not that we don't want relationships to develop; we do. It is just that this is part of the way that we help equip one another for the whole of our lives.

Every leader needs to share that vision. Everyone who joins needs to understand the outcomes that are desired. Nothing can be assumed.

The practice of reading the Bible together

The two practices that most groups will engage in are reading the Bible and prayer. Both are means of encountering God. Both are crucial if we are to form disciples who are confidently following Christ on the frontlines. In terms of discussing Bible passages, group leaders need to know that their task is less about information and more about formation.

One of the ways to help leaders lead Bible studies with an intentional eye on the frontlines of those in the groups is to use the mission framework that was outlined in 'Fruitfulness on the Frontline'. The intention is to move away from generalities to specifics. The temptation for Christians is to deal with abstract intentions rather than link the general commands to real life.

We may all know that we need to 'love our neighbour', but some of us need help to explore what that might mean when our neighbour works in the adjoining office cubicle and is spreading gossip about us with the intention of 'managing us' out of the company. The more we can help one another to make sense of the whole of life, the more these very ordinary, and very painful, situations will be aired together. It will result in a new level of vulnerability that may be challenging for some and group leaders will need to be willing to be vulnerable themselves.

It doesn't avoid the need to wrestle with the text and its meaning, but when thinking through the implications of the text for everyday life, it offers a set of questions that will help to develop an understanding of discipleship in context.

The examples opposite suggest how the text could be linked to frontline lives by linking questions to the 6Ms of 'Fruitfulness on the Frontline' (see Table 1 on page 12).

Modelling godly character	How can this passage shape my character for the frontline? Where are the challenges and encouragements?
Making good work	How does this passage address how I might approach my tasks this week?
Ministering grace and love	Does this passage give me an insight into what grace and love look like? How would this work on my frontline?
Moulding culture	Does the passage give me insights into the culture of the kingdom of God? How would that work out in my frontline contexts?
Mouthpiece for truth and justice	Are there examples in the passage of people taking a stand? What can I learn from that and how can I put it into practice?
Messenger of the gospel	What aspect of the good news is demonstrated in the passage? How does it help me to tell someone else about this good news?

Finally, there needs to be space to help one another stay accountable to their own desires for growth. There are questions that help people be honest about what it means to follow Christ in their particular circumstances. Here are some examples, but there are hundreds that could be used.

- What will we carry away with us into the week from this conversation?
- What will we do differently this week?
- Where might we go that we had not imagined until we were praying?
- What do we need to say and to whom?
- What do we need boldness for?
- What will we stop doing?[9]

The practice of praying together

Praying together is the most helpful thing we can do for one another. It's our shared acknowledgement that we are not all-powerful. It's a public recognition that we get things wrong and we need help to do the right things well. When we know that we are in a safe place to share the joys and struggles of life, it can be brilliantly affirming to hear other people's prayers for us.

But those prayers can also be challenging if they call us back to our core identity as disciples of Jesus.

Often, when I am telling somebody else about the hard time I'm having, what I want them to do is pray for me out of their sympathy. I want someone else to agree that it's not fair, then come to God on my behalf and tell him that it's not fair and ask him to do something about it. I think that is what a lot of our praying for one another in small groups actually amounts to. Our pressure points are shared and we ask God, however eloquent we might try to sound, to take them away.

But there is another way of looking at how we can respond at these times. We could be praying about ways to respond that reflect something of our new life as people in the kingdom. Again, you can use the 6M framework to pray with one another (see the table opposite).

That night when I went to the men's group with all my frustrations about work and family, I looked for sympathy. What I needed was someone to pray that I would continue to be a good worker, a kind team leader and gracious with the public, even when the stress intensified. I needed them to pray that I would be a good father and a better husband. I needed that prayer, and that conversation, even if on the night I might not have wanted to add my 'amen' to that particular prayer.

Modelling godly character	In the context of where we have been this week, how have the fruits of the Spirit been tested in our lives? Which of the fruits of the Spirit would we want to grow in at this moment in our lives? What can we ask God to do?
Making good work	How can we pray for the challenges that we are facing at work and the responsibilities we carry? Can we offer the tasks to God as part of our worship?
Ministering grace and love	Can we pray that we will know how to minister grace and love on our frontline?
Moulding culture	What needs to change? What can only God do? What does he want us to do? Let's pray about both aspects.
Mouthpiece for truth and justice	Do we need to pray for courage and wisdom in knowing when and how to take a stand for truth and justice?
Messenger of the gospel	Who do we want to accept the good news of the gospel? How can we pray for one another that we will do our part so people hear it well?

But if we had prayed together in that way, I would have been reminded that God is not there so we can have easy lives. He is the one we go to in prayer together so that we can be strengthened in our commitment to Christ.

We pray differently when we are trying to help support one another as the missionary people of God.

7. FRIENDSHIPS THAT SUSTAIN US ON THE FRONTLINE

I know what they were thinking about me when we married.

Lucky.

Blessed.

Out of my league.

I've always been the quieter one, she has always been the live-wire. Clever, socially at ease, risk-taking, the one to spot the possibility.

When we settled near the port, we tried to put the past behind us. No-one would want to be forced to leave their own city and keep moving, but at least we could set up a workshop again. I'd always worked with leather and she was great at the business end with the customers.

It wasn't surprising when she struck up a friendship with the fellow from Syria. She is so easy to talk to and he was so interesting. Mostly I just listened.

We became the three amigos, sharing faith and dislocation.

Friends.

Deep friends.

It wasn't hard to find space in the workshop for him and, I have to say, he was quite skilled at working with animal skins. Business was good, but when he said he wanted us to go with him south to Ephesus, it seemed the right thing to do. If we were together, we would be able to really see the mission develop.

And we would be able to help keep him from getting himself into even more trouble than he would if we weren't there to advise him.

Eventually, when he left us in Ephesus, I'm not ashamed to say, I cried. I knew that I would miss him. I'd learnt so much from him and he gave this quiet man a confidence that I hadn't often felt. I felt stronger because he was my friend.

A few years later, we were able to go back home. When Phoebe brought his letter, I have to say, I was quite choked up to see that he had us at the top of the lovely things he said about his friends.

He was right, we had been through so much together. But I don't regret a moment of it. I was so glad that we three had met.

I'm proud that he still calls me, Aquila, his friend.

IT manager, Stephen Landles, had had better days. He was 55 years old, with his long-held dream about to be accomplished. All his office colleagues had called him mad, but he was three days away from Sydney, after sailing from London, when he grounded his boat on a reef and was unable to get it free.

What made it worse was that he had to be rescued by another Brit who was on attachment with the Royal Australian Navy. He pointed out that Stephen had two maps with him. One was accurate and one wasn't. The problem was that Stephen had chosen to take notice of the wrong one.

Once he'd been rescued and was able to reflect on what had happened, he recognized one of the main issues was that he shouldn't have tried to tackle the final leg alone: 'It's good practice to double-check every navigational calculation and you can do that better if you have two independent sets of eyes.'[1]

What he had lacked was someone alongside him. Someone who would be committed to reaching the same destination, aware of the dangers around them, alert to the decisions that needed to be made and willing to stand shoulder to shoulder with him.

Generally, we call that sort of person a friend.

It's what we all need.

When I use the images of the scattered dots (see page 6) to help people get a sense of the significance of their regular contexts as the sites for God to do remarkable things, I sometimes ask how the images make them feel. The range of answers is always interesting. Some will see the potential for influence, the sense of personal significance, the reality of the responsibility to love as 'salt and light'. Then, quite often, someone will talk about a sense of isolation and loneliness.

Of course, they are right to highlight this, because, for many Christians, they are the only ones in their families who are seeking to walk the way of Jesus. They may be the only children in a whole school who worship as part of a church. They may be the only family on the street that acknowledges Jesus as Lord. They may be the only person in the office who would identify as a disciple of Jesus.

That sense of isolation, however, is countered by the knowledge that you have invested time and effort in true friendships. Although people might spend much of their time away from Christian communities, it's encouraging to know that others are supporting them prayerfully, cheering them on in the good times and being willing to listen sensitively on the difficult days. The antidote to isolation cannot be found in busy church programmes; it can only be received in the context of deep friendships.

Peterson describes these relationships in the following way:

Someone enters our life who isn't looking for someone to
use, is leisurely enough to find out what's really going on
in us, is secure enough not to exploit our weakness or attack
our strengths, recognises our inner life and understands the
difficulty of living out our inner convictions, confirms what's
deepest within us. A friend.[2]

It's because I have been so aware of the joy of true friendships
in my own life that I find this so challenging as a church leader.
I want to keep a church moving from merely being friendly
to becoming a church of friends, but this gives me more
headaches than most other things. The headaches are caused
by a mixture of expectation, experience, personality types and
the pressure of time. Mostly, though, the headaches are
caused because I know how significant it is that people do find
friendship in their church community and how hard it is to
achieve.

Defining friendship

Friendship can mean a wide range of different things to
different people. When you listen to some people, they seem
to be able to name-drop scores of people into their conversations, all of them 'friends'. It can be a little dispiriting on the
days when, the numbers of Facebook 'friends' notwith-
standing, you feel like you could count the number of your
friends on one hand. At least part of that difference will be
due to variations in what we mean by 'friendship'.

I want to suggest that if churches are to develop as communities that enable people to grow as confident disciples on
their own frontlines, we need to develop our capacity for true

friendship. These relationships are characterized by offering what you have, and who you are, to another person with 'a radically unlimited liberality'.[3] The goal of this giving, in a Christian context, is not to create some general 'togetherness' or ensure someone's undying obligation. It is so that we can all grow as followers of Jesus. It is one of the primary ways of 'speaking the truth in love' to one another, so that 'we will in all things grow into him who is the Head, that is, Christ' (Ephesians 4:15).

This sort of friendship, a 'holy friendship' has been defined as follows:

> Holy friends are those who, over time, get to know us well enough that they can challenge sins we have come to love, affirm gifts we are afraid to claim, and dream dreams about how we can bear witness to God's kingdom that we otherwise would not have dreamed.[4]

If this idea sounds attractive, the reality is challenging. For those who have been disappointed by previous friendships, there can be an understandable wariness about entering into these relationships again. For those who are busy, the investment of time can seem daunting. For those who are responding to family demands, it is easy to retreat into the circle of 'one's own', rather than offering the gift of yourself to those who may be very different. But the significance is huge.

> Friendship is a much underestimated aspect of spirituality. It's every bit as significant as prayer and fasting. Like the sacramental use of water and bread and wine, friendship takes what's common in human experience and turns it into something holy.[5]

Fundamentally, as C. S. Lewis wrote, we need other people: 'the illusory feeling that it is good for us to be alone is a bad spiritual symptom.'[6]

How friendship shapes us for the frontline

Christian friendship is closely linked to the sense of what sort of human being we want to become. If becoming a Christian is less about agreeing to engage in a set of activities and more about becoming a different sort of person, then friendship has to play into that growth pathway. Friendship is less about offering added pleasure, or relieving loneliness or having someone to share life with, and more about shaping who I can be in Christ. The pleasure, companionship and shared life are enjoyable and life-enhancing, but they are the real added benefits of friendship, rather than the goal of friendships.

I need people who, out of love, will encourage, enable and ensure that I become the best representation of who I can be as a Spirit-filled reflector of God's glory. If they laugh easily, are willing to listen to my flights of fancy and not take me too seriously, I will thank God for the added blessings that I have been given.

Our lives are always lived out in particular contexts. These 'distinct dots' live in particular contexts and degrees of 'greyness'. Friendship is vital to support our intentions as 'distinct dots' – both together in our gathered life and our scattered lives.

Our experience of friendship provides a context for our gathered worship. Most people are not looking for regular anonymous experiences of worship. If someone feels isolated and alienated from the community around them, they are unlikely to thrive or, in most cases, even stay. Although the 'welcome' time or the sharing of the peace might be challenging for some introverts, such acts, incorporated into the fabric of worship, are loud reminders that, although we may come as individuals, we accept the corporate identity of being the people of God, so that we can leave again fully supported by the network of fellow believers.

We want friendships forged in our gathered life to sustain our scattered lives. Our scattered lives are opportunities to serve God's purposes and challenges to stay faithful. To have friends who know where we are, who we are with and what we are doing offers an enviable web of support. The cost of knowing these things is time and active listening. I need to bring my attention to situations that are not mine. I need to try to understand cultures that are alien to my own. I need to remember names, significant dates and the details that will signal this matters. Not only does this change the way I pray for my friends but it also means that I can ask appropriate questions as time goes by.

Fundamentally, I believe that for anyone to stay faithful on their frontlines over the long haul will be remarkably difficult without close friends. As Peterson wrote:

> Lacking confirmation by the word of a friend, our most promising beginnings fizzle. Lacking confirmation in the presence of a friend, our bravest ventures unravel. It's not unusual for any of us to begin something wonderful, and it's not unusual for any of us to do things that are quite good. But it is unusual to continue and to persevere. The difficulties aren't for the most part external but internal – finding the energy and vision to keep the effort going.[7]

SOMETIMES IT LOOKS LIKE THIS

Pat is a teacher in a challenging school and, at times, has struggled with the behaviour of some of the children. Even on a good day, she comes home tired after another day's performance, in time to do some preparation for the next day and so it goes. It would be easy for her not to meet any adults after 6 p.m. until she returned to the staff room next morning.

She has friends. Friends she could call for a chat, friends who invite her out, friends who go back to university days scattered across the country, but she fears that with every passing year her circle of 'active' friends is becoming smaller.

She's part of an average-sized church and, over the summer, approached a number of people she felt safe with to ask if they would be her WhatsApp support group. They are a small group of people, of mixed ages and diverse backgrounds, who were delighted to be asked to support Pat. She contacts them weekly, sometimes more than once, to give them updates on how things have been, how she has been and the answers to prayer that she is seeing.

These people began as supporters, but have become friends. They ask about the effect her job is having on her well-being. They challenge her if they think that she is being too harsh or insufficiently assertive. They are committed to her growth in Christ, so will check with her on her spiritual vitality. They may not go rock climbing with her – Pat's particular passion – nor share her taste in music, but they are totally committed to her and would call themselves her friends. Real friends. People who would drop what they were doing to be available to her. Friends who offer more than they get back. Friends who would never contemplate making that equation.

Friendship in Thessalonica

Whatever Paul may have been accused of, surely it couldn't have been a lack of passion. On occasion, he writes intensely about the nature of the relationships he believes he's had with his churches. In his first letter to the church in Thessalonica, he tries to reassure the readers that he has never tried to deceive the church or use it for his own ends or manipulate the people by blindsiding them with flattery. Nor has he been after their applause. What he has wanted is that they would know they have been loved by him, and he wants to know that they are equally committed to him and they are holding on to the gospel despite all the pressure they are facing (1 Thessalonians 2:3–7; 3:6–13).

Paul had wanted to revisit the church and, for reasons that are lost to us, he was unable to. The pain was such that he describes it as if he were 'orphaned' (1 Thessalonians 2:17). His fear was that the disciples of Jesus in Thessalonica would give in to social pressure and give up on Christ. He was convinced that if he could be with them, he would be able to encourage them, but being unable to get there, he had to send Timothy to strengthen them and encourage them.

It makes me wonder what Timothy actually did when he was with them. I can only imagine it was a range of things that would have involved conversations, prayers, reading Scripture, reminding them of the bigger story they were part of, recollecting the teachings of Paul and passing on the stories of Jesus.

Whatever Timothy did, it seems that Paul need not have worried. The people were holding on to their trust in Jesus; they had not capitulated to the culture around them. That had been his fear. He thought that they would be disorientated by the testing times the apostles were facing and the social pressures they had dealt with when they first became Christians (1 Thessalonians 1:6). Paul's fear was that they would be unable to persevere in a faith that would increasingly isolate them from the wider general culture.

Paul had a strong belief that his friendship and commitment to the Thessalonians would help them stand up to such pressures. This is what Christian friendship looks like. It is more than common interests or general compassionate support; it enables us to hold to the commitments that we have made to Christ. While most of us don't encounter such direct persecution, we do face the temptation to lose the uniqueness of what it means to worship Jesus.

Ultimately, persecution happens to those who do not accept the cultural norms of society. If people will not accept the commonly held belief systems, then they will begin to face pressure to conform. That can happen by being ostracized or ridiculed, though in more extreme cases the pressure will develop into victimization and intimidation. The aim of all this, initially, is to bring people back into line with the wider culture but, as the pressure intensifies, persecution takes on the form of punishment for being different.

If the lordship of Jesus and the kingdom of God are accepted as being radically different from the normal way of encountering life, then it is inevitable that most Christians will face some form of resistance at some stage in their lives. What is needed at times like those are people like Paul and Timothy, friends who are so committed to us that they will do everything they can to come and support us. Following Paul and Timothy's example, their deepest concern will not just be how we are facing the difficult situations but also the extent to which we are managing to continue to be faithful to Christ in the midst of a culture that is shaped by a very different story.

In short, we need friends who are so committed to Christ's ways that they will not allow us to stop following this path of discipleship. We need friends who will stand with us and stand for us as we seek to stand for Christ wherever we might find ourselves. This is not about looking for trouble or developing a persecution complex and it's definitely not about being grouchy or deliberately obtuse. It's the natural outcome of following the drummer who is beating a different rhythm on a different drum. It was one of the things that Jesus promised to those who accepted the challenge to follow him (John 15:18 – 16:11).

IN PRACTICE
Developing friendships that engage the frontline
The desire to help our church develop from a collection of individuals into a community of friends only ever means hard work and frequent disappointment, but it is worth all the effort that it takes. I think there are three three stages involved in enabling this sort of community to develop.

1. Explain the concept
Whenever I meet people who are contemplating joining our church, I try to explain that we want to be a church of friends more than we want to be a church of programmes. I know that programmes can support friendship-building, but we all know that you can have a really great structure of programmes that do not result in friendships being formed. So what does it take to create this friendship-forming and supporting community?

It starts with an explicit awareness of the difficulty of the task. As Carson writes:

> Ideally the church itself is not made up of natural 'friends.' It is made up of natural enemies. What binds us together is not common education, common race, common income levels, common politics, common nationality, common accents, common jobs, or anything of the sort. Christians come together, not because they form a natural collocation, but because they have been saved by Jesus Christ and owe him

a common allegiance. In the light of this common allegiance, in light of the fact that they have all been loved by Jesus himself, they commit themselves to doing what he says – and he commands them to love one another. In this light, they are a band of natural enemies who love one another for Jesus' sake.[8]

That sounds great and, at our best, it is true, but it is this that creates the hard work. The more we have in common, the easier it is to create a community. It is when our horizon is dominated by our differences that community can quickly derail.

True friendship develops in these situations, though – when we don't concentrate on making friends, but accept that we have a shared task together. Lewis explained it like this:

> Lovers are always talking to one another about their love; friends hardly ever talk about their friendship. Lovers are normally face to face, absorbed in each other; friends, side by side, are absorbed in some common interest.[9]

We need to help people accept that they do not join a church, or a small group, to find friends; they find friends when they help one another to learn the way of Jesus together in the midst of all their particular contexts at this stage of their lives. Exploring how friendship develops, Lewis highlights the moment at which that new relationship becomes apparent.

> Friendship arises out of mere companionship when two or more of the companions discover that they have in common some insight or intent or even task which the others do not share, and which, till that moment, each believed to be his own unique treasure (or burden). The typical expression of opening friendship would be something like, 'What? You too? I thought I was the only one.'[10]

As a church, we need to be able to keep our eyes focused on the outcome of our friendship together. We are bound together by and in Christ. In practical terms, if we hadn't come to this church, at this time, we might not have met each other. The relationships develop as we create intentional space for friendship to develop. The meals that we organize to be shared together, the time we spend away together and the connections we create all offer the chance for friendships to grow. But they take on a particular flavour when we recognize that they are the necessary supporting framework for us to live out the implications of the faith, wherever we might be, when we are the scattered church.

If this is an accurate view of Christian friendship, we will need to help one another see both its significance and how it differs from a more general understanding.

2. Commit to the challenge

We need to help people to commit realistically to the challenge of building these relationships and not giving up when the going gets tough.

Central to developing intentional friendships is the somewhat old-fashioned notion that you turn up – even when it is inconvenient, even when you feel that you could be doing something else with your time. You don't bale on your agreements. In a lively, provocative piece in the *New York Times*, Brooks pointed out:

> There was a time, not long ago, when a social commitment was not regarded as a disposable [sticky] note, when people took it as a matter of course that reliability is a core element of treating people well.[11]

We all face the pressure of trying to fit too much into too little time, but if our relationships with one another suffer because we have to keep cancelling, then we lose what we need. Of course, this is easier said than done because it involves swimming against a very strong cultural current. If I am going to be a friend who helps someone else stay faithful to their commitment to Christ, I need to give them the time. There are only so many hours in a day, so I will have to come to terms with the reality that I will not be able to do other things. I will need to commit to the challenge of time.

I'll also have to commit to the challenge of going through painful moments and not giving up. The less you know about people, the easier it is to be friends (though the relationship is probably more accurately one of 'friendly strangers'). When you get to know people, you will find that they are just like you: irritating, surprising, funny, odd, helpful and selfish – the whole bundle of contradictions that typify all of us. It's easy to only pick up on the disappointing aspects of someone else's personality, but if you are prepared to persevere with someone, you may find that they become the person in your life who helps you grow as a Christian.

Dietrich Bonhoeffer led a small community of younger German church leaders just before the Second World War and reflected on the lessons he had learnt in that context. For me, one of the most liberating things he offers is the concept of the need for the 'gift of disillusionment'. He recognized that Christians often approach life in the community with high ideals of what such a community should be like. His view was that the shattering of all those hopes was a result of God's grace, because God will not live in a dream world. He wrote:

By sheer grace, God will not permit us to live even for a brief period in a dream world. He does not abandon us to those rapturous experiences and lofty moods that come over us like a dream. God is not a God of the emotions but the God of truth. Only that fellowship that faces such disillusionment, with all its unhappy and ugly aspects, begins to grasp in faith the promise that is given to it. The sooner this shock of disillusionment comes to an individual and to a community the better for both. . . . He who loves his dream of community more than the Christian community itself becomes a destroyer of the latter, even though his personal intentions may be ever so honest and earnest and sacrificial.[12]

Friendships that sustain our best intentions to be faithful, fruitful disciples of Jesus are created out of who we are. We will never meet the perfect friend; we will only meet people who are willing to come alongside us, as broken as we are. We need to accept that as the gift which is amply sufficient at this time.

3. Practise the art
Finally, we need to help one another practise the art of formative friendship. A church can create a culture where this sort of friendship is normal by developing both signs and symbols alongside intentional practices.

Members of a Baptist church in London emphasized the commitment of the gathered church to support a large proportion of its people on their scattered frontlines as the children and teachers were about to return to school after the summer holidays.

They bought plastic rulers for all the children. The rulers had a simple phrase printed on them: 'We're with you.' There was no church logo, no mention of Jesus and no rainbows! The members of the church wanted every child to feel comfortable enough with the rulers that they would be put it in with the pens and pencils. It was such a simple thing to do, but they wanted the children to understand all that belonging to a church meant. For the teachers they bought stress balls, decorated with the same message and a smiley face.

All-age services allow you to experiment with things that might not be possible elsewhere. In one church, it wasn't hard to organize for someone with a camera and a printer to take pictures of small groups from the congregation that could be turned into key rings before they left the church that day. Carrying an image of someone you have worshipped alongside is not the same as being a friend, but it is a visual reminder that we are connected, even when we are apart.

Of course, on their own, such actions will not create relationships that have the depth we need and they could be seen as tokenistic, so we must ensure that our practices reflect the intention.

As Sheridan and Goheen write:

> The forms of support may vary, depending on context, but certainly should include encouragement, prayer, financial support, insight, and committed wrestling together with scripture as members seek to be nourished in the gospel and bear witness to the gospel in their particular cultural context.[13]

For some, that will be the offer to act as internet accountability partners, which is only possible when there has been enough honesty to know that this is a problematic temptation. For others it will be praying regularly for one another in the light of our particular frontlines. For others it will be the commitment to meet regularly to talk over what is happening in life. It will be different for each person. As leaders, what we can do is ensure that the infrastructure of our life together as a church can point to the fact that we are the church, truly connected to one another whether we are gathered or scattered. For that to be the case we have to know where we are, appreciate the challenges we face and be willing to stand alongside one another sacrificially so that we will stay true to our commitments.

Ultimately, it is not about introducing new programmes, it's about creating communities that are committed to the good news of Jesus so they will gain strength from one another as they share the news in their own networks of friends and acquaintances. The way this becomes a reality is not through events, but by taking one another's ordinary, everyday lives seriously.

All this matters because, as Hauerwas and Willimon suggest, the prize is well worth fighting for:

> The most interesting creative and political solution we Christians have to offer our troubled society are not new laws, advice to Congress, or increased funding for social programmes – although we may find ourselves supporting such national efforts. The most creative social strategy we have to offer is the church. Here we show the world a manner of life the world can never achieve through social coercion or governmental action. We serve the world by showing it something it is not, namely, a place where God is forming a family out of strangers.[14]

Part 3

LEADING GATHERED CHURCH
FOR SCATTERED LIFE

Then the mother of Zebedee's sons came to Jesus with her sons and, kneeling down, asked a favour of him.

'What is it you want?' he asked.

She said, 'Grant that one of these two sons of mine may sit at your right and the other at your left in your kingdom.'

(Matthew 20:21)

What commendable faith and bold planning!

This mother had no doubt that all Jesus had said was going to happen, would happen. Presumably she had been aware of Jesus for years. Maybe she was one of the women who had supported the disciples financially. She wouldn't be the last mother who had to finance her adult children's adventures.

Who can blame her for asking? Who wouldn't want that for their children?

She could imagine a new future.

She trusted Jesus implicitly.

She got it so right – almost.

She could be forgiven for thinking that leadership would continue in the future as she had seen it exercised in the present.

Maybe Jesus nodded towards the Roman soldiers as he said, 'You know that the rulers of the Gentiles lord it over them, and their high officials exercise authority over them. Not so with you' (Matthew 20:25).

There would be a new future.

There would need to be new leaders.

They would just have to be different.

They still do.

What sorts of leaders are able to lead churches that nurture disciples who have a vision for their frontlines?

Different leaders. Leaders who will be successful in shaping the life of the gathered church community to support people in their scattered lives will be ones who learn new patterns of behaviour.

They will be leaders who understand how to develop clear missional partnerships with the whole congregation, who develop the art of perseverance and know how to monitor the progress of developing as a church that sees fruitful Christians operating joyfully on their frontlines.

This section will explore these new perspectives on leadership.

8. ENCOURAGING CLEAR PARTNERSHIPS

It's OK to admit it. I wouldn't be offended.

You wouldn't be the first to have forgotten me – and that's not self-pity.

I really do understand.

I was never a big player. My story wasn't recorded. I can see why. It was never as exciting as other people's.

But I've played my part.

I was there in the early, heady days in Jerusalem. I was particularly moved by Barnabas' generosity. We had grown up in the same place and our families had distant connections. I was pleased to see how he developed into one of the leaders, travelling around encouraging everyone to stay faithful.

When the 'troubles' began, I watched lots of the early disciples leave Jerusalem. I didn't need to leave. I've been blessed. Family money and some wise investments have meant that we have lived comfortably. This large house has been ours for many years now. It's a great place to live and it's big enough to host larger groups of travellers. It's handy for the city and we've enjoyed being able to

*have people stay with us. There have been so many through these
doors.*

*It's how I got to know Peter, Paul and the rest so well. How do
you think Luke heard stories of the early days? We spent many late
nights on the terrace overlooking the olive grove – me reminiscing,
him listening closely.*

I've played my part.

*This has been my contribution to the growth of the church across
the world. Meals, guest rooms and prayer have given me a bigger
picture of the world. I haven't been to most of the places they talk
about, but I know that the gospel is so important to all these people.
It's more than my small worshipping household and the groups of
believers in Jerusalem. It's always been about the wider picture. I
didn't get to see Spain or Ethiopia, but I have always had those
countries in my prayers.*

*All those prayers and gifts offered because I've believed in that
bigger picture.*

*It's been a partnership. I needed them and they needed me.
Together we began to get the job done.*

I've played my part.

'So does this emphasis on the frontline mean that the gathered
church doesn't matter?'

I don't think I've ever been asked this question by people
who spend most of their time scattered on different frontlines
through the week, but I have been asked it regularly by church
leaders, understandably enough.

It's a question that contains a number of other concerns.

- Should all the ministry of the gathered church be about
  scattered living?
- Does this emphasis diminish the role of church
  leaders?

- If we give greater significance to those in frontline settings, do we unintentionally signal that God doesn't call people out of those settings to gathered church ministry?

The answer to all these questions is a resounding 'No'.

What is needed is that the whole people of God – leaders and worshippers – know how to embrace their roles with confidence and how to support one another in their different ministries. We are the body of Christ and 'God has arranged the parts in the body, every one of them, just as he wanted them to be. If they were all one part, where would the body be? As it is, there are many parts, but one body' (1 Corinthians 12:18–20).

Everyone has a part to play in the plans and purposes that God has for this world and we need all to play their parts with confidence and faith. Leadership in this is crucial and it's this role of leadership in the shared partnership of the gospel that will be explored here. But before we explore what this shared ministry might look like, we have to begin by understanding the relationship between leaders and the church they serve.

Leaders need to join their church

'When did you join the church?'

It's an innocuous question that I ask a lot when I am a visiting speaker making small talk with people who have come early before the service begins. It's a conversation-opener, offered in the hope that a longer story will emerge. In my experience, it's not a particularly challenging question. People recall the date and the time of year and they tell stories of who brought them or how they found the building. They recall what was happening in their own lives at the time and the relationships that helped them to be grounded in this community's ongoing life. A simple question.

Unless it's asked of a minister. When asked of them, the variants on the wording suggest something very different. The language of joining is replaced with a more functional phrase: 'So how long have you been here?'

It strikes me that there is a world of difference between 'joining' and 'being here'. Indeed, many church leaders never truly join the church in which they minister. That raises far wider problems which go way beyond semantics.

The difference places us apart from the congregation and suggests permanent transience. We never allow ourselves to belong because we know that we will move again. But if we don't ever join a congregation, the temptation will always be to do things *to* a congregation or *for* a congregation. It will be very difficult to do things *with* a congregation, let alone receive things *from* a congregation.

Too many leaders never join the church they lead.

I want to suggest that if we are to become churches that enable disciples to develop and flourish on their frontlines, we need to embrace a clear partnership between those who are ordained, those who are employed in churches and those who worship together. Specifically, it needs a shared vision for a place, a shared sense of ministry and a shared sense of participation. That will happen most effectively if leaders join their own church.

Leaders need to encourage a bigger vision

They were all in their mid-fifties. Their prospective pastor was in his mid-twenties. The combined number of years' experience of the members of this particular church was 225. His was one day. So the question asked in the interview could have been deemed to be inappropriate or at least premature. Evidently no one had that thought.

He began to answer the question, 'What's your vision for our church?' as best he could. Inevitably, it could only be general because, up until three months ago, he hadn't known where this city was, let alone anything about the church. Inevitably, his was an heroic answer because the church leaders wanted better times ahead than they had yet experienced. So it was hard for him not to follow the unwritten script of a new leader coming in and say that he would increase attendance, improve finances and address the issue of the building.

On reflection, what he should have said was, 'Between you, there are 225 years' experience here. Before I talk about my vision, can you give me a clue as to what is happening already?' But he wanted the job and he was still stuck in heroic mode, so he didn't pause; he pressed on with a don't-worry-the-deputy-messiah-is-here answer.

I got the job.

Looking back on that interview, I think we were all wrong. I think they were wrong to ask someone who had no knowledge of their history to come up with a vision in an interview context. I think I was wrong to play into the heroic leader role. I actually think we were all wrong, too, in what we thought we meant by 'vision'. In retrospect, what we ended up talking about were plans for the church – true vision didn't really come into it.

At a time when there is no shortage of books offering help to develop a church's vision, Sweet's response may be a helpful corrective:

> In one sense, the last thing the church needs is 'more vision'. When Christians sing, 'Be Thou my vision' we are testifying

to the fact that we have all the vision we need in Jesus. Where we need help is in developing a musical ear: ears to recognise the vision that is already at work in the world, ears to hear the future notes, and ears to tune ourselves to God's perfect pitch.[1]

Vision is as much about naming what is as it is about naming what can be. If all our vision-thinking is about our hoped-for future as a church family, we run the risk of dismissing the Biblical vision of the future as well as the present reality of what is happening.

The Bible records a vision of the future that has sustained the people of God down through the generations. It's in the poetry of the Old Testament prophets (for example, Isaiah 65; 66) as well as in the word-pictures of Revelation. It's a vision of the final, all-transformed heaven-come-to-earth existence. It's not through the work of our hands; it is the result of God's own desires. But it does affect us directly because it gives us an idea of the shape of things to come, so we can live into that shape. If God's future does involve security, peace and purpose, then we will seek to replicate those conditions in our workplaces. If God's purpose is to protect the old and the young, we would want to work together to see that become a reality now. If God thinks that it is important enough to have it as a written promise for the future, we are on safe ground in trying to reflect those values today.

When you begin to live into those visions, then the congregational size, financial health and accommodation all begin to look too small to bear the name 'vision'. The vision we have is of God in the wider world, but that can easily fade into generality. The gospel of Jesus is always earthed in a place.

The vision we have is not of a plan for our church but, rather, a vision for the kind of life that God wants for our estate or our town or our city.

What that could look like

Over the past twenty years, there has been a new, growing awareness of the missional potential of churches that work together in unity. Often, there are local networks of church leaders who have prayed together regularly for years. Out of these relationships has come a sense of purpose, whereby churches have been able to develop coordinated, centralized joint initiatives to tackle issues such as drug abuse, financial debt or food poverty, as well as offering events where people can be introduced to Christian faith. The desire to see our cities and towns transformed with the good news of Jesus has transcended the older barriers that divided churches. There are many stories and they are inspiring.[2]

But if these responses to the social needs only include those who can serve in their leisure time or who are employed by churches, then we will not have a true shared vision for the whole people of God. If, instead, we ask where the people of God are throughout the week, where they have been placed by God, then we will see that the whole people of God have a real part to play.

Take an issue like poverty. The grinding challenge of eking out money for another week dominates too many people's lives. It affects their health, their relationships, the future prospects for adults facing it and children born into it.

It's an issue that church-based initiatives have faced head on and they have made real differences. From the 'Faith in the City' report[3] in 1985 through to Christians Against Poverty (CAP), working with those in debt, and the Trussel Trust's development of foodbanks, church-based activities have made a direct and lasting impact in the lives of many. But if churches paused and asked who is aware of poverty in their wider communities and who is in a position to make a difference to those caught in that net every day of the week, they would begin to recognize that it would include so many more people in their congregations.

It would certainly include teachers, transport workers, nurses, doctors, social workers, community workers, clergy, police, shop assistants in supermarkets, volunteers in charity shops, lunch clubs, homeless shelters, foodbanks and neighbours. That is by no means an exhaustive list. The church is engaged with people trapped in poverty, directly and indirectly, in so many different ways.

If we wanted to encourage the people of God to get involved comprehensively with poverty, how might we bring all these people together to hear their experiences and enable them to see how their small piece of the jigsaw is so vital.

If we have a shared vision for our town or city, we will see that it is not just the centralized joint initiatives that matter but also the decentralized joint initiatives. We need CAP centres and all the other brilliant initiatives, but we also want everyone to play their part and to know that their part counts.

The process of arriving at this validation of everyone's ministry could be something like this.

- Our church addresses a social–spiritual need in our local community.
  - *This happens a lot already with great impact.*
- Churches together address a social–spiritual need in our town or city.
  - *This is beginning to happen a lot more often and is good news for everyone.*
- An individual in our church addresses a social–spiritual need in our town or city.
  - *This happens from time to time and new ministries and initiatives are birthed by these passionate individuals.*

- Our church gets behind the mission of an individual addressing the need.
  - *This does not always happen, but often does – especially if the individual is respected in the church community.*
- Churches together get behind the mission of an individual.
  - *This is much rarer, though is more likely to happen if it's an issue such as homelessness or a particular evangelistic ministry, such as ministry to schools.*
- Churches together get behind the mission of groups of their people in their everyday contexts.
  - *I am not aware of this happening anywhere in the UK at the moment, but it could be possible, especially when it is apparent that some towns and cities are dominated by particular industries, so will likely have a number of Christians working there. The city of York, for example, employs many people in the insurance business.*

This is part of the task that church leaders can be involved in. Leaders of a local church can know where people work and what they are engaged in on a daily basis. With other leaders in a town, it is possible that a map could be developed of where people are on a day-by-day basis. This would help everyone to encourage one another that their small contribution was part of a larger picture. They could support one another in the particular pressures that these settings bring. They could celebrate the changes that happen. They could have a fuller vision of what God is doing.

This would be a vision that would reflect the church's identity in both gathered and scattered forms. This is part of the task that church leaders have. As Roxburgh and Romanuk write:

Leadership is about cultivating an environment that innovates and releases the missional imagination present in a community of God's people . . . an environment in which the Spirit-given presence of God's future may emerge among the people of God . . . Missional leadership cultivates an environment in which the people of God imagine a new future rather than one already determined by the leader.[4]

Leaders need a bigger vision and they need to encourage others to have a bigger vision – a vision that is wider than the church and one that sees everyone as having a part to play.

Leaders need to model shared ministry

This has been a constant theme for leaders over the past half century. Generally, though, this refers to the ministry of the gathered church. It has been about widening the core activities so that people's gifts offered to one another are given space to flourish. In different church settings, it has led to teams of preachers, worship leaders, pastoral teams, leadership groups and mission activities. It's not always easy to develop, but it is significant.

But there is an understanding of shared ministry that is wider than that which will usually happen in gathered church contexts.

If we broaden the understanding of the mission of the church, certain things become really clear. The first and most obvious is that there are a lot more people in ministry than we might have imagined. This is potentially liberating for everyone. For those in church leadership holding responsibility for the life of a church community, the outworking of all this work can be measured by more than how many people turn up on a Sunday morning. The ministry of those whose gifts God gave to be offered to the church provide the impetus and content for the life of discipleship that we are called to be involved with. The fruitfulness of those gifts that are offered will be tested in the scattered lives of the church. Your fruit will grow on other people's trees.[5]

Encouraging people to have clarity on the difference between gathered church and scattered living helps to see how God uses all of our contributions. If the gathered church is the network of relationships that primarily help me grow in the ways of Jesus, our scattered lives are the locations where these skills are primarily put to use. In this light, then, we all share in the ministry that God has provided for his world. It begins for all of us with baptism – the mark of belonging to Christ and being wrapped up into his pur- poses – and continues as we find the places where God has called us to serve him at every stage on our lives.

There is a difference btween the roles of leader and worshipper, but they become less significant in this view. Our daily tasks may be different, but we work together for the sake of the world. The Church of England's report, 'Setting God's people free', identified this as key to helping the whole church find its true missional vocation:

> Until laity and clergy are convinced, based on their
> baptismal mutuality, that they are equal in worth and status,
> complementary in gifting and vocation, mutually accountable
> in discipleship, and equal partners in mission, we will never
> form Christian communities that can evangelise the nation.
> The primary sacrament is our baptism in Christ. Both clergy
> and laity are baptised disciples and live out our calling
> together. Lay people – like clergy – have vocations and callings.
> They just happen to be callings and vocations which do not
> require ordination. In this way, clergy and laity are partners in

discipleship. Our paths may sometimes separate to live out our different callings, but they are always aligned, and at times may intersect.[6]

SOMETIMES IT LOOKS LIKE THIS FOR WORSHIPPERS

David and Jane were running four businesses – a farm, a car dealership, a property rental company and a renewable energy initiative – employing around 350 people. But they felt frustrated. They struggled to know whether or not their business life was significant to God.

> We were really wanting to serve God, really wanting to be good Christian ambassadors, but you always feel that you're a failure, you're not witnessing enough, you're not having enough chats at the photocopier. All our staff knew that we were Christians, but we never really had huge opportunities. You can't preach. We were often disappointed in our lack of opportunity to show our faith and it wasn't being addressed in the teaching we were receiving in a big city church. We very much had this sense that we were doing it alone and that, as Christians, we were working things out on the hoof all the time.
>
> Then there was a lightbulb moment. We heard teaching on God's big mission and his purposes for work and we realized that, by running a business employing 400 people and putting wages in the employees' pockets, we were feeding families, preventing poverty. Then you back-fill and we realized that the four core values on which we were operating our business were the most biblical values you could come across. We hadn't actually sat down with the Bible and drawn out some verses, but it was inherent within us, God's creative good order.[7]

The teaching ministry helped them to see their lives differently. They began to see how their business linked with God's widest sense of mission. It was good news for them and is an example of how the different ministries of the church combine together in ways that can help everyone to know their part in God's work.

SOMETIMES IT LOOKS LIKE THIS FOR CHURCH LEADERS

One London vicar recalled a time when he had been called to help someone whose situation was so overwhelming that the person was threatening to commit suicide. For many church leaders this may not be a regular part of their lives, but it is not particularly unusual. What is noteworthy in this story, though, is the awareness that crept up on the leader that he was engaged in his ministry in partnership with the wider church.

> *The police and I managed to gain access to the property before anything dreadful happened, so we began the gentle process of convincing the individual that immediate and proper medical care was needed. In front of the police, the person talked about having faith, but a sense of distance from God. As we all listened, I sensed the challenge of whether or not I would step in and pray then and there in front of the officers. It clearly was not part of their remit, but it was definitely part of mine.*
>
> *I checked that I had the person's permission and, fuelled by a sense of this moment being God's timing, I laid my hand on the person's shoulder and prayed for God's Holy Spirit to strengthen and encourage. Paramedics soon arrived and were able to persuade this dear soul to be assessed professionally at hospital. Things have now improved significantly.*
>
> *Three days later, I was interviewing a policewoman from the congregation during our Sunday evening service. I asked*

her how she felt God used her in her work. To my amazement, she recalled a situation in a completely different part of London where she had attended the home of a troubled person who was becoming aggressive. It was when she had cried out to God, silently in prayer, that the person's attitude suddenly changed and that person agreed to go hospital for the appropriate care.

What struck me was that we were doing very similar work, relying on the same resources and seeing God act in very similar ways. As we have started to explore what it means to serve God on our frontlines, we have found it to be a unifying experience. It's given us a strong feeling of all being in this together.

It's not enough to be aware that there is a shared ministry, there need to be signs and symbols that root this in reality. When leaders are commissioned for their church-based roles, no one can be in any doubt that this is significant work. When we pray for people in work contexts or at those change moments when they take on new responsibilities away from church, we demonstrate that what we have learnt about setting a few people apart for tasks in the church has become an example of what we want to do for the many who serve God's widest purposes. It becomes easier to imagine that we are actually doing this in a shared ministry. But this shared ministry needs a shared plan for it to become a reality.

IN PRACTICE
Leading a process of shared change
Followers of Jesus will agree that their faith should affect how they live, but some find it hard to know what doing so looks like in practice.

Church leaders are not omniscient, so they will probably not know either. The task of leadership is enabling people to understand what God wants of them on their frontlines. Leaders help disciples learn the way of Jesus, in their contexts, at this particular time.

There are three things leaders can do to help that process.

1. Don't rush

If you are in a church that has been very comfortable for people, that has not been very intentional in terms of mission or has not had a tradition of people knowing that frontlines matter or has only celebrated gathered church activities, it is easy to become impatient very quickly. Resist this at all costs. The culture of the church took decades to become what it is and it cannot be overturned overnight. Changes will need to be introduced so that a new culture can develop, but this will take time. I still believe what I wrote in *Imagine Church*: 'Attempts to rush it [change] will either fail or become bullying and manipulative.'[8]

A lack of impatience does not mean a lack of intention, however. In each conversation, you can learn about the joys and challenges faced on different frontlines. As each sermon is being prepared, you can be conscious of the different contexts that people are in day by day. As you fill in events in your diary, you can decide who you want to meet regularly to help them grow as disciples. You may not be in a rush, but you need to be determined to see change.

2. Help people imagine something different

Stories that reflect the experiences of others help people to imagine what could work in their own situations. They help people to see new possibilities. This was illustrated in a recent email received by a colleague.

I work full time as a teacher in a junior school. It's generally a really supportive and positive place to work, but in recent weeks, morale has been low as people have been feeling under pressure and the mood has changed noticeably. One afternoon, four people came in, one after another, to have a moan about others. It was making me sad and I felt a bit helpless to do anything. But then I had a revelation!

I remembered you telling a story about a woman who started to change the culture of her workplace by taking chocolate biscuits into work and wondered if I could do something similar. So, after trying and failing to talk myself out of it, I emailed the staff and invited them to afternoon tea in the staffroom the following Thursday. I was nervous . . . what if no-one came? What if people thought I was ridiculous? In fact, probably my biggest concern was people thinking that I'm a better person than I actually am.

I'd love to tell you that the kingdom broke through in spectacular fashion that day. It didn't, but it did begin to make some inroads, I think. People sat down after a busy and stressful day, had a rest, a piece of cake, chatted and were kind to one another. That's a start, I think. I'll keep praying.

Anyway, I hope that you find some encouragement in this. I'm not sure I would have thought of doing it if I hadn't remembered that story.

Not every story is a huge story; in fact, most aren't. From time to time you may come across the grand, incredible and brave stories of things that happen which have a huge impact. The good thing about them is that you can't miss them as they are so unusual. Enjoy them – they may not be common.

The stories that are more common are ones of normal people, taking normal-people-shaped risks and living to tell the tale. They will be played down by most people involved in them but, as a leader, you have to listen well and remember them. That is the way God works in his own world, through the faithful and faith-filled actions of his people.

Don't dismiss them as too small; encourage them and retell them (with permission!)

3. Help people act differently

When people make small changes, larger changes can result.

We were drinking coffee together and I asked Phil, who worked in the administrative department of a major hospital, 'How's work been this week?' I knew that his department was under severe strain and relationships with management were difficult.

His answer was encouraging and intriguing: 'I did what you suggested and began to pray for the organization. It's strange, but this week has definitely been better.'

Phil is under no illusion that his prayers have solved the pressures in the National Health Service, but he is aware that maybe his prayers have changed his attitude to work. One tweak, one small change – praying – and a man's week began to feel different.

Sometimes the ancient Christian practices of prayer, discernment, generosity and honesty can make all the difference in the wider world. These are not minor practices. They are core to Christian discipleship. Leaders have the privilege of reminding people that they can be confident this way of living will make a difference. The things we do regularly shape the people we become. If we stop to talk to the cleaner each time we pass in the corridor, we become a person who is more likely to notice those who are easily ignored. If we pray regularly for our colleagues, we are likely to care for them.

The shared journey

As we share a sense of vision, ministry and a plan together, there comes a strength from knowing that we are not working alone. It becomes a movement with a cause, fuelled by stories that encourage us to keep going.

If this is how we can start, how do we keep going if we have been on this path for a while? It's the perseverance that will enable the long-term fruitfulness to become established. It is that which we will examine next.

9. DEVELOPING CREATIVE PERSEVERANCE

After a lifetime on the mainland, the island is so small.

I spend most of my time on the headland trying to see the impossible. Some days I think I can catch a glimpse of something in the heat haze, but then it disappears again and I have to accept that, even if I had younger eyes, I wouldn't be able to see anything 30 miles away. But it doesn't stop me looking.

To be honest, I know I'm blessed. I may not be allowed home again, but this is not the worst place that they could have put me. I'm surrounded by those who were once rich, once privileged, once in power. The conversations reflect that. We talk about the government, the corruption and the fear that it will only get worse. They worry about how it will all end.

They took my freedom, but they couldn't stop me worshipping. This day, though, was like no other. I was praying for the churches again, then everything changed. I saw something that shook me to the core.

I was told to start writing. In my mind's eye, I could see each of the churches so clearly. I knew where they were and the pressures

they were under. I could see some of them had become so comfort-
able, accepting the social values of their own cities. I could see some
of them struggling simply to survive.

What I wanted them to see was what I saw: Jesus.

The real ruler.

The real emperor.

The real king.

The one rolling out the scroll of history and taking on the enemies
of all that God intends.

I wanted them to see how everything is included: trade, politics,
suffering, prayers, preaching and worship songs.

Everything.

But they had to keep going. Keep persevering, keeping the faith.
It's too easy to let go.

Please don't give up.

Don't stop believing.

Don't stop praying.

Don't stop speaking.

Don't stop being courageous.

It was a Sunday and I saw the impossible. And I know that it's
true.

John's vision stands as a monumental encouragement to see
everything differently. Every age challenges the Christian
vision of the future. Sometimes the challenge is head on,
through direct persecution. At other times, it comes through
the temptation to slumber, to relax into a gentle accommodation of the surrounding culture.

His message was clear to the church in every age: there is
everything to play for; perseverance will bring its reward.

Leading church so that people are equipped for their
frontlines is enabling people to engage with a culture that
often is at odds with the gospel. It is about ensuring that the

gospel does not remain a personal truth for private lives, but is seen to be relevant in the whole of life.

It is about helping people to be engaged in mission for the whole of their lives. This form of leadership needs creative perseverance. It's easy to revert to a way of thinking of mission as something only engaged in by some people, with the majority of the church being, at best, cheerleaders.

The challenge is how to keep going after there has been some early enthusiasm and appreciation for some new activities that have brought freshness to the lives of the gathered church. This is the story of so many churches that have begun the whole-life discipleship journey. They may have used one of LICC's 'Frontline' resources or introduced 'This Time Tomorrow' (TTT) into some services and preached on whole-life discipleship, but then they get either distracted or uncertain about how to keep the momentum going.

One church leader who is absolutely committed to ministering according to a whole-life perspective said, 'Of course, it's easy to let our focus drift again. Every-member-ministry can too easily be limited to filling up rotas instead of provoking the dispersed ministry of God's people throughout the city.' Allowing ourselves to be pulled back to a gathered church-centred approach to ministry is such a common problem. If it's happened to you, it's not unusual and it's not fatal. There are things to keep you on track, but it takes persistence on everyone's part, especially the leaders in the church. It begins with a persistent posture.

Keep developing the culture

Leaders are primarily disciples. It's their primary identity and their primary vocation. It's their primary posture. Before you were a leader, you were a disciple. When you stop being a leader, you will still be a disciple. Hopefully. We need to model what that looks like as we live out this calling in our contexts. This will be the primary way we help others to see what it might mean in their own situations.

In the early days, trying to encourage, persuade and celebrate fruitfulness on the frontline may feel unnatural and it will take determined planning, precisely because this has not been the thing that has been noticed previously. In many ways, these early days are the interesting and encouraging days. A few 'one-degree shifts' begin to bear fruit and people start to gain a different perspective on their own lives, plus the church as a whole begins to appreciate how its ministry together can make a difference beyond previous expectations. You begin to see the green shoots of change happening.

The next phase is the crucial one. It is after the first year that distractions begin. Because people have been so used to programmes driving the annual agendas of the church, some will want to move to the 'next thing'. Others will have grown tired of the emphasis on the whole of life and will want to introduce other aspects of Christian life. Some will feel that listening to testimonies of people in ordinary life has grown stale and there will be a growing temptation to move away from this.

At this stage, the leaders of the church need to stand firm. They need to ensure that the ministry of the church as a whole stays focused on the goals of whole-life disciplemaking by introducing the initiatives that help to realize the vision and enable the culture to change. There will need to be creativity as different aspects of church life are addressed, but this has to be accompanied by a firm commitment not to move away from a whole-life stance. The fruitfulness of a whole-life-focused ministry may take years to become apparent. As leaders, we are not in control of the pace of other people's growth, but we can trust that if we offer contexts in which people can grow, then there is every chance that they will. What needs to happen is that you stay strong, even on days when others are asking you to change the emphasis of your ministry.

This posture, that seeks to support and equip people as disciples in whatever contexts they find themselves, is seen in the everyday conversations you have far more than in the announcement of a new vision for the church. Once a direction has been agreed, once the frontlines of the congregation are central to the thinking and planning of leadership teams, we get the chance to continue to meet people, ask questions, offer wisdom, pray and support in the everyday conversations. As has been said:

> Leadership is an improvisational act. You may have an overarching vision, clear orienting values and even a strategic plan, but what you actually do from moment to moment cannot be scripted. To be effective, you must respond to what is happening.[1]

It is important to make the planned changes to gathered church activities, but it is equally important to respond to the everyday situations in ways that reinforce people's identity as disciples of Jesus and the possibilities they have to serve God's purposes in the places in which they find themselves.

SOMETIMES IT LOOKS LIKE THIS

One Baptist pastor has made this supporting and equipping posture so natural, it affects everything he is involved with, from the way he views Sunday gatherings through to his everyday conversations.

He describes the sermons as being like a 'half-time team talk: they are an opportunity for the players to be encouraged, refreshed and to gain tactical insight', which will make them more effective as they run back out on to the field of play. But this is not advice from ivory-tower experts. Those involved in leading and/or teaching see themselves as 'player-managers, as they are also actively involved in the game.'

Sometimes, they have specific sermon themes or small group material that focuses exclusively on the frontline, but the awareness that this is the regular context for worshippers means frontline living is something that is part of every service and pretty much every presentation in one way or another.

But it is also present in the incidental conversations that happen through the week. The way that church members communicate with the church office has changed over the past decade or so. In years gone by, members would generally communicate face to face with staff at church-based events or over the phone in the evening or perhaps by letter. Nowadays, people are much more likely to text, call or email while they are actually on their frontlines. Recognizing the reality of these contexts means that, whatever the cause for the communication may have been, he is able to encourage people by assuring them that he will pray for them as he gives them the opportunity to let him know any specific frontline prayer requests.

But he is only too aware of the danger of it slipping away:

There will always be other things that shout for your attention; it is unlikely that anybody is going to call you to account for not doing this! Once you have decided that this is something you want to commit to, you need to have regular reminders to keep going as well as being stimulated to press on in the task of equipping people for their frontlines.[2]

This posture becomes natural only as you persevere in ministering out of these central convictions.

Develop a whole church posture

Years ago, most congregations believed that, in times of crisis (and these would be defined by the people going through the experiences), only a minister's prayers and presence would suffice. It resulted in some ministers burning out while others embraced an heroic understanding of ministry: only the minister was able to help.

That changed as leaders encouraged others to be involved in the pastoral life of the church community.

In emphasizing the significance of leadership in helping to establish a culture of whole-life disciplemaking, there is a real danger that we will replicate this heroic view of ministry. It needs to be heard very clearly by everyone: whole-life support is the work of the whole church, not solely the work of the leaders. The goal of the ministry is:

> to equip the saints as a whole so that the whole church equips itself. . . . The pastor is not the chief equipper of the saints, but rather is one of the many who give leadership to the systemic life of the church so that the church as a whole lives consistently and congruently with its true identity: the people of God invested in the world for Christ and his kingdom.[3]

If the 'systemic life of the church' is going to be shaped around the simple philosophy that the gathered life of the church is for the sake of the scattered people of God, rather than the other way round, leaders need to take a strategic role in making this sit at the heart of everyone's responsibilities.

Otherwise, it is easy to become disheartened.

SOMETIMES IT LOOKS LIKE THIS

Susan knows how that feels. Susan is the pastor of a small, growing church. She has long been committed to whole-life discipleship and had used many of the suggested 'one-degree shifts'. She began to believe that this way of looking at life was beginning to be accepted in her church community. She had invited me to come and help her leadership group take the next steps together in thinking through what this might mean for them as lay leaders in the church.

I'd prepared exercises and discussion questions that would shape the course of the day, but planned to begin by quickly referring to the significance of the dots, scattered and gathered. This was meant to be a reminder exercise, designed to last about ten minutes, so it was an awkward moment when the children's work leader said that she had not really heard this in church before and how liberating it would be if others could hear this message.

Every minister knows how hard it is to stay humble and serene when the congregation responds with overwhelming enthusiasm to something a visiting speaker says when that has been the church's core message over months and years. Susan just about managed it, although I thought that I could see the embarrassment turn to thoughts of murder as she listened to one of her leadership team suggest that this was a brand new perspective.

By the break she had reclaimed enough composure to realize what had happened. The children's work leader had been out of the church services so often, she had heard little of anything. Even when she was in the service, often she was mentally preparing to leave it again to lead her own area of church ministry.

Susan had overestimated how much people pick things up and underestimated how much space and time needs to be

*given to help people see the implications for their own areas
of ministry.*

If we want to move to a position where the posture of a whole church is shaped by a commitment to whole-life discipleship, then as well as introducing the changes to gathered events so people's frontline experiences are highlighted, there needs to be the slow and patient equipping of those who share the responsibility for the ministry of the church. This will include children's and youth leaders, people engaged in pastoral care, small group leaders, those who help lead services and worship teams and those involved in hospitality and welcoming people to church.

The place to start with these people, though, is not with their role in the life of the church. If you do, they may think differently about their responsibilities, but not necessarily recognize the significance for their own lives. If, instead, you begin with how they can see their scattered lives differently and how the gathered church can inspire and support them, they will find it easier to see how their part of the overall ministry can help others.

It's dangerous to assume that people will just get it. It takes deliberate and ongoing input to help people see how to minister differently. Only as that begins to happen will it be clear that the whole church posture is beginning to change.

Keep imagining

The extent to which we will be able to develop whole-life disciplemaking churches will depend on what dominates our imagination. If church as an organization takes up too much room on the horizons of our imagination, we will be unable to see beyond how the church can run more efficiently, smoothly or effectively. If, however, our minds are filled with the simple truth that the church is the people of God, in both gathered and scattered forms, then our imagination will be shaped around thoughts of how these people might be wrapped up into his purpose.

The challenge is that, when many people have experienced most of life as individualists, the prospect of a community in which to belong and find one's place becomes really attractive. So we emphasize the belonging rather than the transform-ation of our hearts and lives that will result in us seeing the whole of our world differently. If that happens, then pastoral ministry becomes needs-focused rather than about equipping people for life.

In a no-holds-barred article, Nicholas Henshill, the Dean of Chelmsford, wrote:

> It is a missiological disaster, in which the priest becomes sheepdog, not shepherd, rounding up an ever smaller flock, and serving the perceived pastoral needs of an entitled and increasingly inward-facing group who have reconstructed worship as the cultivation of an esoteric spirituality rather than the clarion call to community engagement.[4]

One of the themes I keep returning to is that the tasks we set ourselves and the ways in which we conduct those activities will be shaped by the ways we see the people we minister to. If we simply opt for a ministry of sympathy shared with those who suffer, the fruit of that will be minimal – for both the minister and those ministered to. But if we have a bigger vision of what might be possible in the contexts of ordinary frustrations and challenges, there will be so much more at stake. If we keep this in mind, we will want to spend time with people who are seriously trying to make sense of how their lives can become a vocation lived for a wider purpose, regardless of how old they may be. Having a bigger sense of the biblical picture of the church's role in God's economy will help us to shape our own work.

In Ephesians 3:10, Paul outlined the significance of the church when he wrote:

> His intent was that now, through the church, the manifold wisdom of God should be made known to the rulers and authorities in the heavenly realms, according to his eternal purpose that he accomplished in Christ Jesus our Lord.

That full sentence raises so many significant questions. What is this manifold wisdom? Who are the rulers and authorities? Where are the heavenly realms? What is God's eternal purpose that was accomplished in Christ?

The clues to the answers to these questions lie in the rest of the epistle, although the specifics are debated among Christians. At the risk of seeming overly simplistic, though, the significance of this for us is not to understand what effect we may have or, indeed, if we are affecting anything at all. The significant question is how the church can make plain the manifold wisdom of God.

Wisdom in the Old Testament is the art of living with a profound sense of God's desires for the whole world. It is about creating and sustaining wise order and avoiding the conflicts that bring disruption. It's about how we speak *to* one another, *about* one another and *on behalf* of one another. It's about how we use our wealth and power for the sake of others. It's about how we see businesses develop so that they are beacons of good news for a whole society. It's about how we bring up children and include outsiders in our family networks and create places of safety and security.

Ultimately, God's wisdom is perfectly demonstrated in Jesus, who brought people together to form churches – outposts of the kingdom – as living contrasts to the prevailing rulers and authorities. These rulers and authorities 'always tend to marginalise or kill people or groups who don't fit their narrow band of acceptability. The church is to be, by the very fact of its existence, a warning to them that their time is up, and an announcement to the world that there is a different way to be human'.[5]

For this to be seen, it seems obvious that Paul must have had more in mind than their weekly gatherings. The diversity of their worship services was significant when much of society was divided on class or racial lines, but God's wisdom would be seen not solely in worship but would be 'made manifest' in the crucible of the monotony of daily routines.[6]

Paul's letter paints a dynamic picture of how belonging to one another in Christ would make a difference to their lives in their own society. We need the same faith-washed imagination for the lives of all those who believe themselves to be part of the church.

We need to see where people are, to help them to see what it means to follow our King, Jesus, there and support and encourage them when that commitment leads them to be pressured to conform. This is the imagination we need to keep feeding.

This can sound heavy, but it can be demonstrated by the ways in which we acknowledge the transition moments in the year.

SOMETIMES IT LOOKS LIKE THIS

In many churches, there's a second 'new year' moment that happens in September. As the final days of August roll by, thoughts turn to going back to school. The roads get busier as parents drop children off at the school gates or with childminders. Even for adults, the change from the summer holiday season to autumn feels like a time to re-enter the world of work with another burst of intentionality.

One of the ways that some churches have begun to mark that moment is by holding a 'Blessing of the backpacks' within one of their late-August to early-September services. It can become an occasion for all the church, regardless of age.

We were all very excited about the blessing of the backpacks service. Johnny was thrilled to be back at school last week and happily put on his backpack as if going to school. Edward can't wait to start in Reception next week and asks every day if he can go to school today. Bertie is very excited to be joining Nursery and was beyond proud to take his brand-new book bag to church this morning. It was an inspiring way to reset, put the holidays behind us and prepare for a new term and school year.

As for me, I started a new job last week after taking a year out. I held up my shiny new mobile phone. I want to do things differently this time. I really want to hear God's voice, when I hit a snag in the office, before I act, rather than seeking forgiveness after I act, for less-than-Christian thoughts and behaviours.

I want God with me at work, not just on Sundays. Thanks to today's service, every time I look at my mobile I'm going to be reminded of God's blessing. . . . Maybe my few hours a week at my desk are the mustard seeds – the little moments that might not feel like a lot, but have the power to change things. So, while I attend 'Blessing of the backpacks' with certain trepidation thinking, 'Well, I only do x, y, and z', I keep going back to the day of small things, the small beginnings. Because maybe they hold the seeds of blessing.[7]

Perseverance's fruit

Paul's perspective was that a life of faithful perseverance produces character, which, in turn, produces hope (Romans 5:4).
We know that this is how perseverance works – in any area of
life. It shapes us in certain ways, it forms character, because we
are willing to be patient and resilient in the face of challenges
and disappointments. It creates a sense of purpose about our
conversations and plans. We are willing to take the long view
and recognize that change takes time, but is worth the effort.
Paul's final goal was hope – hope that doesn't disappoint.

In terms of shaping congregations that together equip one
another for fruitful lives, there needs to be a sense of not
being rushed while at the same time being purposeful. There
will be many times when 'mid-course corrections' will
be needed. There will be seasons when it becomes obvious
that the cause has to be re-presented. Every new person
joining the church and the leadership groups will need to be
able to see the significance of all that is involved. This is
persistent, determined ministry for the long haul.

It is also good work. It's working with the grain of God's
desires for his own people that we will be shaped to be more
like Christ and less like our surrounding culture. It may be
slow, patient work, but it is work that is worth engaging with.
What will be needed along the way will be some sense of how
much progress is being made. This is what we turn to in the
next chapter: how will you know if you are making any
progress at all?

IN PRACTICE
The value of frontline visits
One of the practices that helps leaders persevere is the making
of appointments to meet people on their frontlines. If you go

with an open mind and are curious enough, it is rare not
to find things that evidence the grace of God. Once you find
these, not only will you be encouraged but so will the people
you visit. You are demonstrating that you will not give up
believing that God is at work in these places, no matter what they
might believe.

Some leaders have expressed concerns about what to say
or do in these contexts. Essentially, it is more about listening,
less about saying or doing things, so the need is to have access
to questions that will open the door for conversation.

Of course, if a person's primary frontline is his or her work,
you might not be able to go into the workplace, for all sorts of
reasons, but you could commute with him or her or meet nearby
for lunch or a drink after work. By going there, you are creating
a profound symbol of your commitment to that person.

1. The set-up.
   - Begin with someone you already have a rapport with.
   - Make it as convenient as possible for the person in
     question.
   - Where possible, meet in the actual place of work or
     in the immediate vicinity.
   - Don't stay too long! Agree the timings . . . and leave
     when you said you would.
2. Ask good questions. Here are a few to get you started.
   - What is your job title?
   - What does your job entail?
   - What opportunities are there to offer Christian values
     or influence what happens in your workplace?
   - What challenges have you faced in your workplace
     because of your work?
   - How have you experienced God in your work in the past?
     Where is he in the present?

- How is your experience of work shaping you as a follower of Jesus?
- What brings you joy here?
- What helps you keep going? What could the church do to help you more?
3. Pray for all you hear. Ask how you can pray . . . and do pray for them, there and then!

Change can happen, but change that counts takes time. As a leader, I cannot allow myself to be frustrated by that. As the next chapter will explore, there are ways to take note of how things are changing, as well as trusting the one who causes things to grow.

10. CLARIFYING CONSTANT PROGRESS

We loved listening to him.

Sometimes he'd really make us laugh. You had to be there to hear his talent for timing the punchline.

Other times you could hear the intake of breath and, just when you thought you knew where his stories were going, he'd introduce the twist at the end. And it would leave you a bit disorientated. Things didn't end the way you thought they would.

We loved listening to him because we can't tell them like he did. I could repeat what he said, but it's not the same. He said it so much better.

We're just ordinary.

Not much going for us; we get by.

We can grow stuff and I can cook fairly well. We are Mr and Mrs Average, I guess.

But he knows us.

Truth is, he's one of us.

I know his mum well. I've known him since he was a boy and he knows me.

So when he saw us standing in the crowd on the shore, I'm almost certain he winked at me as he talked about a woman baking bread, measuring out the flour carefully, then adding the yeast and working it into the flour really well until she was sure that the dough would rise in the oven.

You don't need a lot of yeast to make bread that feeds a whole family.

You don't need a lot of seed to fill a field with wheat that supplies a whole village.

What struck me was that he was speaking to my neighbours, some of whom, to be honest, are hopeless in the breadmaking department. It's a good job they only have a small field because I think they'd struggle with anything bigger.

But it doesn't matter how good you are, does it?

It matters if the yeast has gone off.

It matters if the tiny seeds are missing.

As long as you have yeast and seeds, things happen.

Even for the least talented of us.

Even for the ordinary folk like us.

We are just a baker and a farmer.

But we see growth.

For anyone who is trying to change things for the good of others in any context, the question that haunts us is: how do you know if you are making any progress at all? For churches and leadership teams who are seeking to make disciples living purposefully on their frontlines, these questions will crop up time and time again.

- How is it going?
- How can you be so sure?
- Have you any evidence for what you are claiming?

They are good questions and they need to be responded to head on. To do that, though, we first need to take time to work out what we are actually trying to answer.

What we are trying to do

On the simplest, most basic level, what I am proposing is that the way we help one another to serve God's purpose in our own places is by taking one another's lives really seriously. It sounds so simple, but when we encourage people to see that they are precious to God, regardless of abilities, strength or age, and are wrapped into God's purposes, we are encouraging them to take their own lives seriously. We are saying we want to help you do that.

When we encourage one another to embrace the places where we spend most of our time as the places that God has put us to live out the difference that following Jesus makes, we are taking one another seriously. When we help one another embrace those places when they are not where we would *like* to be, we are taking one another's lives seriously.

When we help one another to grow in wisdom and confidence as we respond to situations in a godly way and make Spirit-creative things happen because we find courage, we are helping one another take our lives seriously.

When we resolutely believe that, whatever stage of life we are in, God will give his gifts and use us for his purpose, and we pray for one another, we are taking one another seriously.

This is what we are doing for one another, together.

We are helping one another to see that the gospel may appear to be as small as a seed, but it can make a huge difference. We are helping one another to see that acting out the values of the kingdom, as insignificant as they may seem, can affect so much more than we might have imagined.

Measuring progress

Some leaders will argue that it's wrong to even begin to try and measure what is happening. They will want to remind us that we are not dealing with an industrial, mechanical production model. The Christian life is not simply the result of A + B = C. Life is far more complicated than that. We are all different personalities, with different experiences, at different stages of life. Discipleship, as we have stressed throughout the book, is not a programmatic response to life and it cannot be developed simply by engaging in any one particular programme. We grow as disciples as we increasingly recognize who God is and learn how to live life as 'a journey you must travel with a deep consciousness of God' (1 Peter 1:18, MSG). I have a lot of sympathy for this view.

In the same way, just as I think it would be weird to sit down with my wife on our wedding anniversary and fill out a questionnaire to see if we had grown closer emotionally, I think it is equally strange to think that I can use any such similar blunt instrument to gauge my life with God. Life is not that simple. Relationships are not that simple. Questionnaires are not that good.

In my marriage, however, I might want to take notice of whether we have laughed more this year than cried. I might be able to look back at my calendar and see how I spent my time. I might be able to recall the difficult situations we navigated with greater ease than we have done in the past. These reflections might improve my sense of the health of my relationship with my wife.[1]

In a similar way, as a leader of a church committed to helping disciples learn the ways of Jesus, I may notice the stories of people acting in countercultural ways at work. I might become aware of them forming new friendships as they take time to develop relationships with people in their frontline settings. I may remember shared conversations that suggest people are becoming increasingly honest about faith and how they have been able to share that with others.

In other words, I may not be able to measure things on a chart, but I could tell you some stories that might indicate ways I feel we are growing as followers of Jesus.

I wonder if the problem lies with the language of measuring. It suggests numbers and charts and even that we will fall into the target-driven culture which, at times, cripples many areas of work. If, instead, we move from the expectations of mechanical monitoring to noticing how things develop organically, we might become alert to things that are important. Certainly, if we were to ask what we are able to notice around us, that would lead to different conversations.

If, as church leaders, we think of ourselves more like farmers than business managers, we would see ourselves as the distributors of seeds. The promise of growth is in the seeds rather than in the farmer. The farmer's job is to try and ensure that the land is prepared to receive the seeds, but, that aside, all farmers need to concentrate on is ensuring that the seeds are scattered liberally enough to give a good chance of any growth at all.

After the sowing of the seeds, the farmer can chase off the vermin and opportunists that would try to steal the seeds, but mostly the farmer will watch to see the landscape change. An empty field will change as things grow. Every stage of that growth will bring reassurance, relief and threat. Things could go badly wrong at each stage. The rain could be too heavy or there could be a drought. The temperature could drop to freezing and kill off the early growth. The sun could burn the tender new shoots. Hidden disease could cause the loss of the whole crop. Nonetheless, there is a chance that farmers will get to the day when, climbing into the harvester, they know this is what it was all leading towards. The crop may well be what was expected, in line with the seeds that were scattered, though the exact shape, size and quantity will be a surprise. But it can all be celebrated.

Growth is to be expected. Health does lead to more or better growth but, ultimately, we are not in control of the yield. If we are faithful in our sowing, we can be confident that some things will grow. What, how, where and the degree of that growth will, however, be beyond our control.

But we can remain confident that growth will happen. After all, if farmers didn't think that growth was a possibility, why would they get out of bed in the morning?

What is measurable

The easiest things to monitor are the inputs that have been made to the existing church's life. So, for example:

- it's a simple process to note how many TTT stories have been shared over a year;
- you will know how many visits you have made to meet people on their frontlines;
- you will be aware of how many times, when preparing sermons, you have consciously read the text through the lens of the scattered church;
- you will know if the church's midweek groups have had the chance to use resources that encourage them to think about their frontlines;
- you will remember if you have publicly prayed for people who have started new jobs or taken on new responsibilities;

- you will be conscious of the conversations you may have had with worship leaders or children's workers or those involved in pastoral care to help them see how their areas of ministry can equip people for frontline living.

And so the list can develop. This sort of monitoring is straightforward because it relates to things that a minister or a leadership group has had some control over.

The more difficult thing to know is what difference this has made in the lives of those who worship together week by week. Although it may be difficult to gather this, if it is done, we will be more aware of how things are changing for people.

There are three principles that lie behind this desire to assess change.

First, it will have to be a study of the changes that happen over time rather than relying on simple snapshots. The individual stories are encouraging and give people the opportunity to think of ways that they can act differently in their own situations. Indeed, that has been the intention behind my inclusion of the stories in this book. They are not models but, hopefully, they are encouraging examples. They can show that something has been grasped, something has happened. If, though, we want to know whether or not real change has happened, we will have to be patient and watch what happens over a longer period of time.

The adoption of new habits takes time and the outcomes of those new habits take further time. You cannot be in a rush with all this. Of course, that doesn't mean you sit back and just hope for the best. You trust the seeds of the whole-life gospel, you prepare the ground, you encourage the growth and you make sure that pests and disease don't interfere with that growth. But you know that the harvest will take time to come.

Second, you need to be as aware of the distance travelled as you are of the destination reached. For some people, the whole idea of living intentional lives of discipleship that result in changed actions, reactions and responses to the world around us is one that may be new to them. Be gracious with people and help them to take the steps that are appropriate for them at their stage of the journey. For others, their experience of church and Christianity may have been an engaged enthusiasm, but it has all been church-centred rather than focused on their whole-life contexts. Again, you will want to be alert to the disorientating feelings that they might have when they realize the extent of the division between their sacred and secular lives, which they have been encouraged to embrace up to this point. In every case, change is possible, but patience and grace are needed.

Third, you must expect to see changes develop. It sounds obvious, but some leaders who have been engaged in church ministry have been so frustrated by the lack of change that they stop believing it is possible. We can't forcibly change hearts, we can't make people follow Jesus, we can't insist that they seek out ways to serve God's purposes in their own contexts, but we can pray. Prayer is not the action of last resort; it's foundational to all that we have been outlining here because, ultimately, this is God's work that we are helping with, not our work that we are asking God to help us with.

From the moment that Jesus began his public ministry, his primary strategy was to get the good news of the kingdom out to the villages, towns and cities by recruiting a group of people who he would teach, train and send to act and speak for him. If we are right in suggesting that this strategy has never changed, then, when we pray, we can be confident that we are working with the grain of God's own desire.

Appreciating the growth

Many organizations have used Appreciative Inquiry as a tool to help them reflect on their life together. Put simply, the approach is one that concentrates on what is going well, rather than focusing on what is challenging. The wording of the headline questions that are used is along the following lines:

- what is – concentrating on all that is going well;
- what could be – the openness to future possibilities;
- what will be – what do we want to commit to seeing develop?

This happens best in conversations rather than in written surveys. If you have a large church context, however, then it might be better to have a mix of the two: quantitative and qualitative reflections. The following questions were used in a large church after the leaders had been emphasizing whole-life discipleship for a number of years. They give an indication of their approach. For each of the questions, there was a sliding scale for responses (from 1 to 5).

1. All of the leaders of our church understand that a major aspect of our mission as a church is outworked through the everyday lives of our members.
   What evidence would you offer or what stories could you tell to support your answer? [This was included for each question.]
2. As leaders, we have created a strategy for envisioning, equipping and inspiring our members as whole-life disciples.
3. We have taught and occasionally revisit the vision of being a 6M disciple.

4. All members of our church know what we mean by their 'frontline' and know what it means to live there faithfully.
5. We have implemented a number of 'one-degree shifts' in our church, to support the whole-life discipleship vision.
6. Whole-life discipleship is acknowledged and featured within our main worship gatherings.
7. When people meet in small groups or other smaller groupings, there is the opportunity to discuss and pray for issues relating to their frontlines.
8. The preaching in our churches helps people to connect Scripture with the reality of their frontline lives.
9. Our printed publications (newsletters, prayer bulletins and magazines) feature people's frontline lives.
10. As leaders, we try to listen for, capture and share stories from people's frontlines.

There were also some questions that were used in conversations. Again, they included a sliding scale for responses, this time from 'strongly disagree' to 'strongly agree'.

1. I understand clearly what is meant by a frontline.
2. I am committed to serving God in all aspects of my daily life.
3. I am growing in understanding of what God wants me to do in my everyday contexts.
4. I pray for the people and circumstances that I encounter on my frontline.
5. My church envisions, equips and inspires me to live faithfully for God in my daily life.
6. I am developing habits of prayer and reading that sustain my intention of growing in the ways of Jesus.

Following the 6Ms of 'Fruitfulness on the Frontline' (see Table 1 on page 12) that have been highlighted in the church, each aspect was explored as follows.

7. *Modelling godly character*: I am self-consciously responding to people and circumstances on my frontline in ways that reflect the fruit of the Spirit.
8. *Making good work*: I seek to undertake every task – at work, home and play – as though I was working for Christ alone.
9. *Ministering grace and love:* I regularly find myself going the extra mile for others, even those I don't necessarily see eye to eye with.
10. *Moulding culture*: I have managed to find ways to make changes for the better on my frontline, bringing it more in line with how God would like it to be.
11. *Mouthpiece for truth and justice*: I have been willing to grasp the nettle and stand up for truth, fairness and kindness on my frontline.
12. *Messenger of the gospel*: I have been able to share why I trust in Jesus with one or more people on my frontline.

These questions are examples of how one church has tried to chart its own life. The questions can be modified. The conversations are the key element and the sense that people are able to develop their own confidence in living their lives as disciples of Jesus.

Maintaining confidence

What if, despite our best efforts at leadership, nothing changes in your church? What if, despite our best efforts in our scattered lives, nothing seems to change? Have we failed?

We are called to live in ways that reflect what we believe to be true. As leaders, we have to minister in the light of who we understand God's people to be. If we face resistance – and, from time to time, we will – that should not change our course of action. The community of people we belong to deserve more than leaders who are primarily concerned about popularity rather than a good cause. The mission situation we face in the UK is serious. Too many people have never knowingly encountered the gospel of Jesus, which will make sense of their whole lives. If the church does not come to terms with the obvious fact that all our activities are not for our own sake, things will not change. It is not enough to continue to lead churches that are self-serving or, at best, have only a minority engaged in mission. We need to help the whole community of God's people to see that they can be used by God for his agenda. If people resist this idea, that's one thing, but to stop challenging and encouraging them to live as disciples would be failure.

Similarly, living out the implications of the gospel in every area of life will not automatically mean that we will see 'success'. Other people may not be persuaded by the demonstration of what a whole-life expression of Christianity offers. That workplace culture may not change from its ruthless and driven character. Again, that does not mean we have failed.

Both leaders and people have played their parts. Together we recognize that we are called to be faithful because, for all our planting and tending, it is God who actually makes things grow. There will be opposition from the enemy of God's good plans and sometimes setbacks will occur on our watch. That does not mean we have failed either. It simply means that we were faithful and there are many promises of rewards for faithfulness because faithfulness never seems to be good enough in our eyes. That's why eternity will be full of surprises.

SOMETIMES IT LOOKS LIKE THIS

What does it look like when all the pieces come together, when leaders and people are able to work together and both get the chance to see how God can take their specific offerings and make something out of them all?

Arnie is an athletics coach.

When the people of his church began to concentrate on the significance of one another's frontlines, a number of things fell into place for him. He began to realize that God is just as much concerned about and involved in what we do Monday to Saturday as he is on Sunday.

> For me, it clarified that everything I do, even when I don't realize it, can be hugely significant for the development of the kingdom of God.

This new-found frontline focus led to a deepening of his relationship with God. Whereas before he had believed that God was not majorly involved in what he was doing during the week, he began to approach the beginning of each week with a profound sense that God was with him, God was doing things in and through him and God loved it when Arnie partnered with him in what he was doing.

Arnie explained:

> I now feel much less pressure to [evangelize] everyone . . . I feel like God is calling me to genuinely love people, to befriend them and to allow the opportunities to speak about him to come up in a more natural way.

Now he sees his job as that of being somebody who points people towards the kingdom and helps them to move closer to it, but does not feel pressure to force people in. Without even realizing it, he had been living with so much guilt, but now this has dissipated.

At the same time as this shift took place in Arnie's thinking, he and his home group benefited from something that seems so simple, but at the same time is quite revolutionary: they have made a conscious effort to see one another on their own frontlines.

On one occasion, the church's curate, a member of the home group, came to visit Arnie at the athletics track, where he was coaching hurdles. While the curate was talking to a group of teenagers, Arnie was at the other end of the track doing some one-to-one coaching. The girl he was working with asked who the curate was and why he was there. Arnie explained that he had come to see what he does and to pray for him.

On hearing this, the girl asked what it meant to pray, which opened up a great conversation about what it means to live in relationship with God and to involve him in our daily lives. She then asked Arnie, 'Do you pray for me?' to which he answered, 'Yes.' By now, she was really intrigued and asked, 'What sorts of things do you pray for?' Arnie was then able to walk her through an example of a prayer. She was both amazed and very grateful. Having had this conversation, Arnie is now regularly able to share with her that he's praying for her about various aspects of her life and the conversation continues.

It's the joy of persistence.

The wisdom of the farmer

Being a city dweller, I have no direct experience of the life of a farmer. All I can do is imagine myself in that situation. But

aspects of farming become vividly applicable to me when I
apply them to our church community. My anxiety is not about
failed crops, inclement weather and crop-killing pests and
diseases, it's about Christians wrecking their faith, struggling
with major life situations and being lured away by temptation.
I have those fears most weeks.

I need the wisdom found on a farm. I need the wisdom that
comes from reflections in first-century Palestine:

> He [Jesus] also said, 'This is what the kingdom of God is like.
> A man scatters seed on the ground. Night and day, whether
> he sleeps or gets up, the seed sprouts and grows, though he
> does not know how. All by itself the soil produces corn –
> first the stalk, then the ear, then the full grain in the ear.
> As soon as the corn is ripe, he puts the sickle to it, because
> the harvest has come.'
> (Mark 4:26–29)

The confidence of the farmer who decides that he might as
well sleep because the seeds will do their work contrasts with
so much of my own sleep-disturbed nights. We are involved
in something so much bigger than just trying to help people
get a bigger vision for their own lives or helping a church
experience renewal. It's all part of the kingdom of God,
the actions we take together with God for the blessing of the
many.

Another farmer, this one in twentieth-century Kentucky,
reminds me, though, that farmers also can change, as can
leaders. This desire for fruitful growth affects everyone,
including the leaders who oversee the fields.

> Don't worry and fret about the crops. After you have done all
> you can for them, let them stand in the weather on their own.

If the crop of any one year was all, a man would have to cut his throat every time it hailed.

But the *real* products of any year's work are the farmer's mind and the cropland itself.

If he raises a crop at the cost of belittling himself and diminishing the ground, he has gained nothing. He will have to begin over again the next spring, worse off than before.

Let him receive the season's increment into his mind. Let him work it into the soil.

The finest growth that farmland can produce is a careful farmer.[2]

The prayer, then, becomes that all this work – this good work of creating fruitful communities – will create careful leaders. Leaders who take care of the message, take care of the lives of those they worship alongside and take care of their own lives.

So may it be.

NOTES

Preface

1. See, for example, LICC's 'Transforming work' resources, along with the weekly emails, 'Word for the Week' and 'Connecting with Culture' (available at: <www.licc.org.uk>, accessed 15 February 2019).

Introduction

1. Mark Greene, *Fruitfulness on the Frontline* (Nottingham: IVP, 2014).

1. The invitation to whole-life discipleship

1. Dorothy Sayers, 'Why Work?'. This was originally delivered at Eastbourne, England, April 23, 1942 (available online at: <http://tnl.org/wp-content/uploads/Why-Work-Dorothy-Sayers.pdf>, accessed 12 March 2018). It is also included in *Letters to a Diminished Church* (Nashville, TN: Thomas Nelson, 2004).

2. David Ford, *The Shape of Living: Spiritual directions for everyday life* (Grand Rapids, MI: Zondervan, 2002), p. 30.

3. Frederick Dale Bruner, *Matthew: The churchbook,
   Matthew 13–28* (Grand Rapids, MI: Eerdmans, 2004),
   p. 811.
4. Tom Wright, *Paul: A Biography* (London: SPCK, 2018),
   pp. 290–291.
5. Lucy Peppiatt, *The Disciple: On becoming truly human*
   (Eugene, OR: Cascade, 2012), p. 79.
6. Graham Cray, Foreword in Neil Hudson, *Imagine Church:
   Releasing whole-life disciples* (Nottingham: IVP, 2012), p. 13.

2. Developing vision for everyday disciples

1. R. Alistair Campbell, *'Born Again': What did Jesus mean?*
   (Cambridge: Grove Books, 2012).
2. Marianne Meye Thompson, *John: A Commentary* (Louisville,
   KY: Westminster John Knox, 2015), p. 325.
3. Laura McBride, *We Are Called to Rise* (London: Simon &
   Schuster, 2014), p. 197.
4. It's hard not to read our understanding of the awful atrocities
   of the transatlantic slave trade or modern-day slavery into
   the pastoral epistles. Slavery was never good news for those
   enslaved, but there were noticeable differences at the time
   Paul was writing. For example, slaves could buy their freedom
   or, at least, under Roman law, expect to be freed by the age
   of thirty. For an overview of slavery in the time of Paul, see
   A. A. Rupprecht, 'Slave, slavery', in Gerald F. Hawthorne,
   Ralph P. Martin, David G. Reid, *Dictionary of Paul and his
   Letters* (Downers Grove, IL: InterVarsity Press, 1993),
   pp. 881–883.

3. Discovering the joy of frontline mission

1. Steven Garber, *Visions of Vocation* (Downers Grove, IL:
   InterVarsity Press, 2014), p. 189.
2. Tony Hendra, *Father Joe* (London: Penguin, 2004), p. 55.

4. Worship that inspires us for the frontline

1. Michael Rock, 'Human emotion: the one thing the internet can't buy', *New York Times*, 14 October, 2015 (available online at: <www.nytimes.com/2015/10/14/t-magazine/human-emotion-the-one-thing-the-internet-cant-buy.html?mcubz=0>, accessed 12 October 2017).

2. Scot McKnight, 'Spiritual eroticism', *Christianity Today*, May 2009 (available online at: <www.christianitytoday.com/pastors/2009/may-online-only/scot-mcknight-spiritual-eroticism.html>, accessed 15 April 2018).

3. The key work in this section reflects the theology and ideas contained in Sam and Sara Hargreaves' book, *Whole Life Worship* (London: IVP, 2017).

4. Kent Anderson, *A Spirituality of Listening: Living what we hear* (Downers Grove, IL: InterVarsity Press, 2016), p. 153.

5. Hargreaves, *Whole Life Worship*, p. 27.

6. Hargreaves, *Whole Life Worship*, pp. 30–39.

7. See LICC's website for more resource ideas (available at: <www.licc.org.uk/resources/whole-life-worship-downloads/>, accessed 15 February 2019).

8. Eugene H. Peterson, *As Kingfishers Catch Fire: A conversation on the ways of God formed by the words of God* (London: Hodder & Stoughton, 2017), p. 272.

9. Hargreaves, *Whole Life Worship*; LICC's website (available at: <www.licc.org.uk>, accessed 15 February 2019).

5. Preaching that equips us for the frontline

1. This section includes some of the insights that were shared in 'Whole Life Preaching'. See LICC's website for this resource, designed to be used, ideally, by groups of preachers (available at: <www.licc.org.uk/resources/preaching>, accessed 15 February 2019).

2. I chose these references fairly randomly. Once a reader becomes alert to the way that God is seen in everyday situations, you realize there are examples on most pages of the Old Testament.

3. In this case, Kenneth E. Bailey, *Poet and Peasant and Through Peasant Eyes* (Grand Rapids, MI: Eerdmans, 1983), pp. 119–141.

4. Bailey, *Poet and Peasant and Through Peasant Eyes*, p. 122.

6. Small groups that encourage us for the frontline

1. Roger Walton, *Disciples Together: Discipleship, formation and small groups* (London: SCM Press, 2014), p. 151.

2. Walton, *Disciples Together*, p. 112.

3. Walton, *Disciples Together*, p. 113.

4. Walton, *Disciples Together*, p. 113.

5. Walton, *Disciples Together*, p. 114.

6. Richard T. France, *Matthew* (Leicester: IVP, 1985), p. 276.

7. This section has been very influenced by the insights offered by Peter Oakes, *Reading Romans in Pompeii: Paul's letter at ground level* (London: SPCK, 2009), pp. 98–126.

8. Of course, we don't know the answers to these questions. Oakes writes (p. 105), 'In a house church one might have expected roles to be allocated by the householder of highest status, who would also tend to be the church's host. Paul takes away that prerogative. It is not apparent how the church was to discern which gifts each member had. However, Paul clearly intends it to be a "charismatic" process under the control of God, not a person. We do not know how radically the ministries were distributed.'

9. There is, of course, a rich tradition of such questions, not least Wesley's questions for his Band meetings:

   1. What known sins have you committed since our last meeting?

2. What temptations have you met with?

3. How were you delivered?

4. What have you thought, said, or done, of which you doubt whether it be sin or not?

5. Have you nothing you desire to keep secret?

These questions are explored in depth in D. Michael Henderson, *John Wesley's Class Meetings: A model for making disciples* (Nairobi: Evangel Publishing House, 1997), pp. 118–119.

7. Friendships that sustain us on the frontline

1. Mark Chipperfield, 'I took a wrong turn says sailor stuck on a reef', *Daily Telegraph*, 3 August 2007 (available online at: <www.pressreader.com/uk/the-daily-telegraph/20070803/281822869400991>, accessed 9 November 2017).

2. Eugene H. Peterson, *Leap Over a Wall: Earthly spirituality for everyday Christians* (New York: HarperCollins, 1997), p. 54.

3. Helmut Gollwitzer, *Karl Barth: Church dogmatics: a selection* (Louisville, KY: Westminster John Knox Press, 1994), p. 173.

4. L. Gregory Jones and Kevin R. Armstrong, *Resurrecting Excellence: Shaping faithful Christian ministry* (Grand Rapids, MI: Eerdmans, 2006), p. 65.

5. Peterson, *Leap Over a Wall*, p. 53.

6. Clive S. Lewis, *The Four Loves* (London: Collins, 1963), p. 8.

7. Peterson, *Leap Over a Wall*, p. 55.

8. D. A. Carson, *Love in Hard Places* (Wheaton, IL: Crossway, 2002), p. 61.

9. Lewis, *The Four Loves*, p. 58.

10. Lewis, *The Four Loves*, pp. 61–62.

11. David Brooks, 'The golden age of bailing', *New York Times*, 7 July 2017 (available online at: <www.nytimes.com/2017/07/07/opinion/the-golden-age-of-bailing.html?_r=0>, accessed 2 February 2018).

12. Dietrich Bonhoeffer, *Life Together* (New York: Harper & Row, 1954), p. 27.

13. Timothy Sheridan and Michael Goheen, 'Missional spirituality and cultural engagement' in N. A. Finn and K. S. Whitfield (eds), *Spirituality for the Sent: Casting a new vision for the missional church* (Downers Grove, IL: InterVarsity Press, 2017), p. 112.

14. Stanley Hauerwas and William Willimon, *Resident Aliens: Life in the Christian colony* (Nashville, TN: Abingdon, 1989), pp. 82–83.

8. Encouraging clear partnerships

1. Leonard Sweet, *Summoned to Lead* (Grand Rapids, MI: Zondervan, 2009), pp. 14–15.

2. Roger Sutton (ed.), *A Gathering Momentum: Stories of Christian unity transforming our towns and cities* (Watford: Instant Apostle, 2017).

3. Archbishop of Canterbury's Commission on Urban Priority Areas, *Faith in the City: A call for action by Church and nation: Report of the Archbishop of Canterbury's Commission on Urban Priority Areas* (London: Church House Publishing, 1985).

4. Alan Roxburgh and Fred Romanuk, *The Missional Leader* (San Francisco: Jossey-Bass, 2006), pp. 5, 9, 42, quoted in David Heywood, *Kingdom Learning: Experiential and reflective approaches to Christian formation* (London: SCM Press, 2017), p. 159.

5. Kate Shellnutt, 'Remembering Bob Buford, the Christian leader's leader', *Christianity Today*, 19 April 2018 (available online at: <www.christianitytoday.com/news/2018/april/bob-buford-died-leadership-network-halftime-peter-drucker.html>, accessed 20 May 2018).

6. Lay Leadership Task Group, 'Setting God's people free: A report from the Archbishops' Council, February 2017,

GS 2056, p. 4 (available online at: <www.churchofengland.
org/sites/default/files/2017-11/gs-2056-setting-gods-people-
free.pdf>, accessed 15 February 2019).

7. Lay Leadership Task Group, 'Setting God's people free', p. 8.
8. Neil Hudson, *Imagine Church: Releasing whole-life disciples*
   (Nottingham: IVP, 2012), p. 39. The whole book outlined a
   change process for those who wanted to set out on nurturing
   a whole-life disciplemaking church.

9. Developing creative perseverance

1. Ronald Heifetz and Marty Linsky, *Leadership on the Line:
   Staying alive through the dangers of leading* (Boston, MA:
   Harvard Business School Press, 2002), p. 73.
2. The Revd Ken Benjamin in conversation with Joe Warton,
   March 2018.
3. R. Paul Stevens and Phil Collins, *The Equipping Pastor*
   (Washington, DC: The Alban Institute: 1993), pp. 75–76.
4. Nicholas Henshall, 'Shepherds turned into sheepdogs',
   Church Times, 21 July 2017, p. 13.
5. Tom Wright, *Paul for Everyone: The prison letters* (London:
   SPCK, 2002), p. 36.
6. Tish Harrison Warren, *Liturgy of the Ordinary: Sacred practices
   in everyday life* (Downers Grove, IL: InterVarsity Press, 2016),
   p. 292.
7. Debbie Clinton, '430 commissioned during blessing
   of the backpacks at All Saints Fulham', Diocese of London,
   27 September 2016 (available online at: <www.london.
   anglican.org/articles/430-commissioned-blessing-backpacks-
   saints-fulham>, accessed 20 April 2018).

10. Clarifying constant progress

1. Of course, I could ask my wife, but I fear that might result
   in a different answer!

2. Wendell Berry, 'Prayers and sayings of the mad farmer'
   in *Collected Poems: 1957–1982* (New York: North Point Press,
   1985), p. 131.

ACKNOWLEDGMENTS

It ends with thanks.

When this book is published and I talk about it to others, I will call it 'my book', though, of course, it will never be just my book. It's the product of so many other people's thoughts, wisdom, experiences and help.

I've been part of a fantastic community of people working together at LICC for over twelve years. As a team, they are some of the most supportive and kind people I know. They have prayed regularly for this book, asked how I have been getting on and generally cheered me along the way. I am blessed to have been part of this wider team of people.

A subset of that wider team has been the Church Team: Stefan McNally, Steve Rouse, Andrew Belfield, Joe Warton, Lindsey Caplan and, until recently, David Lawrence. They have been hugely significant in shaping many of the ideas here. They have worked with hundreds of church leaders and leadership teams around the country, helping many to begin this long journey of their church communities becoming

whole-life disciplemaking churches. It's been a privilege to
lead this team of gifted leaders.

Mark Greene, LICC's Executive Director and Tracy
Cotterell, the Managing Director, have made major contributions to this work, as well as my wider work. They have
provided inspiration, encouragement, focus, shaping hands
and creative eyes on what I have done. They are great to work
for and with. They make you want to do well.

Until recently, when he went to become a pastor in the
North West, Antony Billington was my first port of call for
any new thoughts, however fuzzy they were. He has spent
hours listening with kindness, trying hard not to roll his eyes
or point out too quickly that my new thought was, in fact,
commonplace thinking. He has an eagle eye for details.
Without his careful editing there would have been some
major typos! And without him I would have laughed far
less often.

For all the members of the churches we have had the
privilege of getting to know, the church leaders we have
walked alongside and the individuals who shared their stories
with us and gave us permission to share them with others –
thanks ever so much. Sometimes it's easy to wonder what will
become of the church in the UK. No one knows. But what I
do know is that there are some stunning examples of godly,
creative and loving people around the place. God's not
finished with us yet.

For the various people who contribute to LICC's cause and
the trusts that have funded my post over the years, thank you
for the faith you have shown in us. You make a difference and
we are very grateful.

My own church community is Salford Elim Church. A
better church family you could not wish to find. I've been part
of this community for such a long time now. The people here

have supported me in all I have done with prayer and encouragement. When you find the people in a church love you that much, you know it is home. It has been. It will be.

Finally to Maggie, my wife. She's the one who reminds me that life is more than church and I am more than a church leader. She's great. I'm glad I'm married to her! Together with Beth and Oliver, Joel and Rachel, she doesn't really care that I've written a book. They are much more interested in whether or not I am becoming a more fully rounded human being – a whole-life disciple. They are absolutely right. At the end of the day, that's what counts.